HOOKED ON HOOPS

Understanding Black Youths' Blind Devotion to Basketball

by
Kevin McNutt

CHICAGO, ILLINOIS

Front Cover illustration by Ed Bunche
Copyright © 2002 by Kevin McNutt
First Edition, First Printing

HOOKED ON HOOPS
UNDERSTANDING BLACK YOUTHS' BLIND
DEVOTION TO BASKETBALL

ACKNOWLEDGEMENT

Colossians 3:17
"And whatsoever we do in word or deed, do all in the name of the Lord Jesus, giving thanks to God."
Hebrews 13:15
"By him therefore let us offer the sacrifice of praise to God continually, that is, the fruit of our lips giving thanks to his name."

My Lord and Savior Jesus Christ provided me every word, idea, and experience. I am merely the tool He has used. As his proud servant, I accept this and give all glory and honor to Him.

I would like to thank the pastor of my church, From the Heart Church Ministries, John A. Cherry, and his family for their wisdom, teaching, and disciplined articulation of God's word and ways. Their courage and vision were instrumental to my motivation to write this book.

I would like to thank the hundreds of coaches, players, parents, adults, teachers, administrators, teammates, opponents and fans of basketball on all levels, for how they have touched and shaped my basketball life and made this book a reality. There is no way I can name everyone that moved my heart and stimulated my passion for basketball, and more importantly accelerated my desire to hopefully empower young athletes through this book.

I was inspired by: A lecture from a teacher in the fourth grade; an interview heard on radio between a Black athlete and White commentator; a coach that kicked me out of practice for a lethargic effort; an opponent's intentional elbow to my ribs on a drive to the basket; a stunned and confused look by a White potential employer thinking that by my last name and earlier phone interview that I was a blue eyed Irish American; a group of young Black players, which brought defeat with them to the court but now, frustrated by another soon to be loss, literally cry and blame the officials, especially me, for cheating them; a genuine, respectful, and honest "thank you, sir" from a Black ballplayer from "the hood" as I took a moment to talk to him instead of possibly banishing him from the game as emotions rose during an intense contest. All were just as instrumental in molding this book as the on-the-record, off-the-record interviews, conversations, phone calls, lunches and dinners, locker room discussions and roundtable forums with all those I have known and come in contact with during my 45 years on this Earth.

I especially want to thank the Black community, particularly those passionate about sports and its relationship with the Black athlete. One thing I came to understand perfectly clear–the Black community has the answers, manpower, resources and expertise to empower itself to overcome and change any obstacle. We are blessed with brilliant, resourceful, creative, caring and energetic people within our sports culture and community. We only need a better focus and an increased understanding of the value of networking. Everything else needed to force change is in place.

As Allen Iverson so dutifully and respectfully states after another 40-point night while leading his team to victory, I too want to "thank my teammates" for all their help. Desiree, my loving wife; Monica and Melanie McNutt, my daughters; Lang Reese; Dan Cronin; Valerie Keels; Terri Anderson-Robinson; Rosalina Bray; Ken Shropshire; Kevin Jackson. These people, and many other family members and friends "fed me the rock" so that I could put up the "big numbers." Their patience and sharing were instrumental and essential to the completion of this project. I will always remember how their active participation, technical and computer assistance, general support, opinionated dialog, suggestions, pep talks, selfless encouragement, vision, and unabashed joy for my success helped keep me marching toward the goal.

My publisher, Dr. Jawanza Kunjufu is a beautiful and special man. His vision and intellect, courage and pride made *Hooked on Hoops* a reality. I thank God for him. He reached out and took a chance on my dream when others did not. Perhaps, as a Black man and Black athlete (he ran track for Illinois State), he could relate to the subject matter in ways that others could not. Equally as important as the chance he took on publishing my manuscript, I would like to thank him for the invaluable discussions and directions he provided to me. Always patient always understated yet on point, Dr. Kunjufu forced me to take the extra lap or run the extra sprint to express and organize my thoughts and writings; To reach back and be sure that I was taking the last shot in the development and articulation of the story told in *Hooked on Hoops*. Our relationship has a special coach-player bond.

Lastly, in the Washington DC-Baltimore corridor, I implore all families, students, and schools to attend The Great Blacks In Wax Museum in Baltimore city. Whenever I vacillated on the value of this book, the museum was the adrenaline shot to boost my energy levels. I have been to the museum five times and counting. I learn more about my history and myself with each visit.

DEDICATION

To my wife, Desiree
Proverbs 18:22
"Whoso findeth a wife findeth a good thing, and obtaineth favour of the Lord."

And my daughters, Monica and Melanie
Psalm 127:3
"Lo, children are an heritage of the Lord: and the fruit of the womb is his reward."

Love, Always

HOOKED ON HOOPS
UNDERSTANDING BLACK YOUTHS'
BLIND DEVOTION TO BASKETBALL

INTRODUCTION

When Michael Jordan hit the game winning jumper from nineteen feet to beat the Utah Jazz in game Six of the 1998 NBA Finals it cemented his name as the greatest player of all time. It also inflated his already larger than life status within the Black community and the world. To be like Mike was already the dream of young athletes around the globe. Now the dream was taking flight to a new level. Imagine hitting the last shot of the NBA finals to win the championship as the world watched. Then to calmly retire from the game as a six-time NBA champion comfortable in the knowledge that your last shot was a made basket to win the NBA title. Hollywood could not produce a better ending.

If the odds of a high school athlete playing sports professionally are one in 10,000, the chances of a Black athlete walking away from basketball on his own terms must be 1,000,000 to one. In the Black community, youth grow up wanting to be Michael Jordan. They want to be a professional athlete. They love sports and basketball in particular. But what they don't understand is that basketball will quit them before they will quit basketball. Jordan's last second shot to win the championship and his subsequent retirement (on his terms), while at the top of his game, was truly a one-in-a-million dream come true scenario. In reality, it almost never happens that way—not even for Michael Jordan.

Despite his basketball legacy and successful business ventures off the court, including part ownership of the Washington Wizards and position as President of the team, Michael Jordan, citing a "love for the game" returned to the NBA as a player in 2001 following a three year retirement. While it is unlikely that Jordan can duplicate another dream scenario such as the 1998 game winning, championship-series-determining, last-second shot, we can only hope that he will leave the game on his terms instead of the game quitting on him. But what a great lesson to illustrate to young people specifically Black youth and the Black sports community, with the emphasis on the captivating and love/addictive relationship of basketball than the return of Jordan to the sport. If the Black community was ever confused about just how irresistible basketball can be, his return is Exhibit A.

Black youth who are committed to becoming professional athletes need to understand that basketball without a corresponding dream of success away from the game is nothing more than a train wreck waiting to happen. Most athletes are jilted by basketball early in their athletic life. They get cut from their middle school tryouts. They fail to make the high school team. Some eventually make the team, but ride the bench in high school. These players transfer to another school only to find the new program a duplicate of the first. The majority of Black athletes are not offered a college scholarship. They play junior college ball, but again are not offered a scholarship to a Division I school. In college, a few players briefly earn a starting position on the team, but are replaced by newly recruited, more talented players. They get suspended from their college team. They tear up a knee and never regain their old form. They fail to get drafted by the NBA. They fail to get invited to an NBA camp as a free agent. Still others make an NBA roster but are cut or traded. They try to hang on to sign just one more contract, one more hefty payday, but management decides that now is the time to go—leading to a forced retirement. These are among the ways basketball will quit on you before you can quit the game. For every Michael Jordan or John Elway, who left football after leading the Denver Broncos to victory in the 1999 Super Bowl, there are millions more that will be forced from the game before their mind and ego tell them they are ready.

Black athletes, in particular, need to take heed of this situation for they are usually the athletes that sell out totally for the game. They are the athletes *Hooked on Hoops*. The danger is when the ball stops bouncing they do not have an alternate plan to fall back on. It is why the Black athlete's fall from basketball prominence is such a steep and immense drop, greater than any other ethnic group in a given sport. There are a myriad of reasons that lead to the Black athlete's all-or-nothing relationship with basketball. It has its roots in the Black culture where he is raised, a culture that places an inordinate amount of praise and value on successful Black athletes. Society's overall account and perception of the Black athlete's worth and capabilities is also a contributing factor to the dilemma. His own problems of inferiority and self-esteem factor into this equation. He has a total misunderstanding of what the game of basketball or sports in general should be in relation to the rest of his life. He has a blind trust that sports, primarily basketball, will always provide him with purpose, adulation, visibility, respect and wealth. This same trust allows some from within his culture and others from outside his community to prey on his devotion to the game and pigeonhole him into a total commitment to his sport while they reap the benefits. All of these factors have merit as to why the Black athlete is consumed with sports and particularly a professional sports career.

Hooked On Hoops takes an in-depth look at the Black athlete and his roller coaster ride with basketball. The book intends to show how the game of basketball can have so much positive value on so many different levels of the Black athlete's life, yet when abused or overindulged can have a negative aftermath.

Hooked on Hoops emphasizes the need for the Black athlete, parent, and community to seek wisdom and knowledge about the games we play. From youth league to Amateur Athletic Union (AAU). From the local newspaper to "March Madness". From an all Black high school basketball team at a private school to sports that are almost totally void of Black athletic participation. Instead of espousing playing, cheering and celebrating the game in our typical, merry, happy go lucky, nonchalant manner, *Hooked on Hoops* attempts to hit the pause button with the jump shot in mid-flight and ask the difficult question of why.

Why are Black youth drawn to basketball? Why do we substitute basketball for educational attainment? Why does the Black community have such an infatuation with Black athletic success? Why does the Black athlete dominate basketball and football but is almost non-existent in so many other sports? Why don't we care about other sports and instead seem so content with participating only in basketball and football?

To answer these tough questions, *Hooked on Hoops* focuses on the plight of Black youth, where the spectra of sports, and basketball, in particular, are catastrophically out of proportion with reality. Witness a 1996-97 survey conducted by Northeastern University's Center for the Study of Sport in Society, which stated that 66 percent of Black males between the ages of 13 and 18 believe they will earn a living playing professional sports. The figure is more than double the proportion of young White males that have the same thought. Further fueling this out of control inferno is the fact that Black parents are four times more likely than White parents to think that their child will have a professional sports career. While the data is alarming and cause for serious analysis and concern, it is incomplete in terms of understanding the addictive and one-sided relationship between the Black athlete and sports.

One thing that has become abundantly clear to me after almost 40 years of playing and officiating basketball in the big city is the fact that the pursuit of an NBA career is not the primary problem facing Black athletes. In fact, those that believe and speak about the NBA dream as the central cause of the Black athlete's plight betray a shortsighted, automatic, distant, and casual concern for the predicament of the Black athlete. The NBA dream is a symptom of the problem. It is no different than any of the other symptoms faced by the Black athlete, including poverty, lack of exposure, low expectations, stereotyping, lack of ethnic pride, racism, exploitation, greed, lack of knowledge about our history, our culture's obsession with sports and sports participation, and the lack of value placed on education. In truth, the dominant problem is how sports tyrannize the Black male, perhaps like no other institution in this country.

Hooked on Hoops uses basketball in the big city and surrounding area to generate critical thought and insight. There is no other game that descriptively defines the relationship between the Black athlete and sport. The goal of the book is to inform and provide clarity about sports, particularly basketball, and Black youth participation.

As a former athlete, I played basketball on several levels including playground, high school varsity, summer league, college, and adult recreation league for 20 years within the metropolitan area of Washington DC. For the last 17 years I participated in many of these same leagues again, but now as a referee. I have also coached on the high school level. And while all are noteworthy, equally as important is the fact that I used basketball to earn a college scholarship and graduate from George Mason University in four years. Sure, like most Black athletes from the big city, I chased the "dream" and basketball painfully quit on me before I was ready. But the result of my relationship with basketball was a college degree which provided a springboard to a success (including writing this book) that I had never envisioned while going one-on-one and launching jumpshots on the playground. While I can understand why the Black athlete chases the professional dream, I cringe over how we squander our educational opportunities. I have a unique perspective and insight into basketball concerning how and why the Black athlete plays the game with such passion and the resulting consequences.

CHAPTER ONE:
The Resilient Black Athlete

The high school basketball coach stood and motioned emphatically for his 5'8" point guard to come to him at the bench. The young Black athlete hustled at the request of his coach. Coach Richard Jackson, a robust, dark skinned Black man, had a pained expression on his face and with arms open wide and palms up, almost pleading for clarity, asked his star player, "What are you doing out on the floor?"

As the referee in this game, I watched this encounter as the other players on the court lined up for free throw attempts. I had officiated games with Coach Jackson's team, Phelps Vocational High school in northeast Washington DC several times over the previous couple of seasons. His teams were well organized, disciplined, intense, smart, played with purpose, and were winners despite not having a player on the roster over 6'3". I respected Coach Jackson and his teams and he respected and appreciated me as a referee.

Tonight's game was a quarterfinal playoff game and emotions were at a higher level than normal. In the playoffs, you move on with a win but with a loss the season and perhaps, in the case of seniors, your athletic career is over. Still, for the most part, it was another faceless game between two Black big city teams in front of a sparse but enthusiastic crowd in a seemingly forgotten corner of northeast Washington DC. Yet, to the athletes on the floor it was the equivalent of the Final Four.

Not waiting for a response to his initial question, Coach Jackson asked his star guard how he could allow the ball to be taken from him resulting in free throw attempts for the other team. The star guard, visibly frustrated, replied that he was fouled on the play allowing the steal by the defender. Coach Jackson had complained earlier in the game about the physical tone of the contest. Now seeing the sincerity in the eyes of his star guard, the coach decided to defend his player as he ushered him to a position back on the floor.

1

Next, in his baritone voice heard throughout the gym and primarily addressed to the officials he exclaimed, "Yeah, I know! We are getting killed out there but keep playing!"

Having watched the exchange and understanding his response, I said nothing and the game continued. Shortly thereafter during another free throw situation, I stood next to Coach Jackson and casually said, "Killed, huh? That's a pretty strong statement." Coach Jackson paused and then glancing at me with a sheepish smile said, "You make a good point Mr. Ref. I understand."

At the time of this game, Washington DC was often called the "Murder Capital of America." One of the local television stations featured a program entitled "City Under Siege" every night after the 10 o'clock news detailing crime incidents in Washington DC. Mostly, under siege were Black youth and Black men. Consequently, our brief dialog is my favorite and most meaningful exchange ever with a coach in a game situation. Two Black men in authority positions acknowledged, first, their love for Black youth, and second, that the plight of the Black male athlete is far greater than any basketball game.

Oh, how I yearn and bleed for our community to seek a proper relationship with basketball and sports in general, a relationship where basketball is used by the Black athlete instead of basketball using the Black athlete. I wonder if it can ever happen. If Black youth are to find a balance with sports, and basketball in particular, adult leaders must show the way. This is why I valued my interaction with Coach Jackson. Yet, the attitudes, decisions, and perceptions of adult leadership regarding the Black athlete's plight in sports, especially basketball, are so encased in covert, overt and institutional racism, self-hate and low ethnic value, blinded by media stereotyping and cultural ignorance, and enhanced by greed, apathy, and timidity that Black youth ultimately are left confused. They are channeled toward sports that at least they know will provide them with a definitive (win-lose) conclusion. In other words, while adults continue to play their political games surrounding Black athletes their decisions impact youth devoted to sports in real and tangible ways.

* Apathy and Overt Discrimination *

Conditions are so deplorable and unsafe at many of the high school gyms in Washington DC that had this been an area other than a city with a 75 percent Black population many facilities probably would have been condemned. The schools' athletic budget is 50 to 60 percent less than neighboring, mostly White Montgomery (MD) and Fairfax (VA) counties. Washington DC is no different from most urban cities. Educational spending in urban cities with predominately Black enrollments is often far less than their counterparts in the suburbs. Equity in education will never happen until the 2 to 1 ratio of dollars often allocated for spending between the urban city and suburbs is narrowed.

At Phelps Vocational School in northeast Washington DC, the gym also substituted as the stage. At one end of the court, approximately four to six feet beyond the basket, was a four-foot high wood paneled stage. Players that drove to the basket with too much momentum either had to dive onto the stage or slide into it to stop themselves. Both were very dangerous and players could very easily be seriously hurt. At the other end of the court, the landing area behind the basket was probably less than four feet before athletes would collide with a concrete wall that was without padding. Yet, for how atrocious these safety issues appeared there was still one that was even more dangerous. As I back-pedaled down court during a fast break, I tripped and almost fell over what I thought was another player's leg or foot.

During a stoppage in play I inspected the area only to notice a two-inch wide, inch and a half deep groove in the floor. Apparently, the seam was for an accordion curtain that separated the room. Why there was no strip to cover the floor is anybody's guess.

Regardless, the result was that any athlete could have gotten a shoe caught and shredded the ligaments and cartilage in his knee or ankle possibly ending his career. I didn't know how many games had been played at the facility in the past but the next morning after the game I reported my concerns to Dr. Allen Chin, the Executive Director of DC Public Schools Athletics.

* Covert Discrimination *

The basketball officials association that has jurisdiction over Washington DC and neighboring Montgomery County Maryland is IAABO Board 12. The board has over 250 referees. Yet annually, Dr. Chin is disgusted with the quality of referees and the service that is provided by Board 12 and in particular assigning commissioner of officials, Joe Marosy. Board 12 has refused to meet all of the basketball needs of Dr. Chin and his public schools. For example, Marosy, who is White, will not send referees to cover middle school and junior high basketball games in the city. Marosy claims he does not have enough referees to cover the 3:30 start of the games. Yet, games starting at the same time in predominately White Montgomery County are well stocked with capable referees.

Most likely, the real reason is that many of the referees (mostly White, some Black) are fearful for their safety and prefer not to go into the city, especially into the allegedly rough neighborhoods in Southeast and Northeast. In addition, the games pay less, require leaving work early, and lack prestige in relation to a high school game, which are covered by the media. They are without the same security and police presence and are largely for the benefit of invisible Black youth. Meanwhile, Dr. Chin is forced to solicit the support of grass roots referee organizations to work the games. It is a poor substitute. The organizations, mostly Black, have good intentions. But with makeshift rosters short on manpower, the games are often played with one referee, without referees, or sometimes with

The Resilient Black Athlete

referees totally unequipped to handle the talent, pace, and intensity of big city youth basketball.

* Institutional Exploitation *

Approximately three out of every four Black male athletes that played Division I-A college basketball at America's predominately White colleges and universities failed to graduate from these institutions. The abysmal data has been compiled and released publicly by the NCAA. Recent 2001 data revealed that only 24 percent of Black basketball athletes that entered college as freshmen in 1994 at 114 reporting Division I-A schools, graduated from the institution six years later. Overall, the graduation rate for the Black athlete at the 319 schools competing in Division I basketball was 35 percent.

Some colleges cite the Black athlete's addictive focus toward an NBA career and poor academic backgrounds that leave them ill-prepared to handle college coursework as the primary reasons for the poor graduation rates. While there is validity to these charges the problem is far more complex. Perhaps a more prevalent, yet rarely discussed, explanation is the volatile combination of big business college athletics and the mind-boggling "culture shock" experienced by Black athletes as they attempt to adjust to an entirely different academic, social and racial environment. As Black athletes are lifted from their surroundings at age 17 and 18 and asked to assimilate to the high pressure atmosphere with its production mode mentality, and the social isolation of the college climate, many athletes simply find the experience overwhelming. Mainstream society, meanwhile, is unsympathetic. They would tell the Black athlete that the college environment is better than where you came from so get over it. I often wonder if they were White athletes at predominately Black schools whether there would be such a harsh judgment of their academic success or lack there of. I am sure racial sensitivity training and cultural diversity courses would be mandatory for faculty, administrators, students, and athletes.

The issue of racial isolation is real. Of the 297 schools (excluding the 22 historically Black colleges and universities, or HBCU) playing Division I basketball in 2000–2001, approximately 56 percent of these schools had Black student enrollments of less than seven percent. Yet, most of these schools have basketball teams and starting five units dominated by Black players. In the power basketball conferences including the ACC, Big East, Southeastern, Big 12, Big 10, PAC 10, Atlantic 10, and Conference USA, over 75 percent of its projected starters in the two-year period from 1997-98 and 1998-99 were Black players. Many teams fielded all Black starting line-ups. Clearly, in college basketball Black gold means recruiting and having Black athletes. In the 2001 Final Four, 18 of the 20 starters for Duke, Arizona, Maryland and Michigan St. were Black athletes. Meanwhile, the NCAA has signed a $6 billion 11-year contract with CBS Sports to televise college basketball featuring March Madness and the NCAA tournament.

Make no mistake about it, the Black athlete prep superstar now on campus feels the pressure and intensity of the big business nature of college basketball. First, he, his parents and many within the Black community fail to understand the fine print of the college scholarship, believing it to be a four-year guaranteed commitment from the university. It is a huge misinterpretation.

The athletic scholarship is for one academic year only. It may or may not be renewed at the end of the academic calendar year on or before July 1. This must be done each year. The decision to renew or cancel an athlete's financial aid is left to the discretion of the university (read: coach and athletic department).

Black athletes on campus quickly learn that basketball has been elevated to a cold, calculating, employee-employer relationship short on excuses and focused entirely on athletic productivity and output. For the first time in their athletic lives many athletes have to make an inward assessment of their skills. This is something they have never had to do in their previously glorified hooked on hoops relationship with basketball. The Black athlete finds himself in a situation unique to any other student on campus; combined with adjusting to a new social, academic and racial environment, he must question his skills under the unremitting glare of the scholarship committee.

* Lack of Self-Empowerment *

While racial isolation is a valid and legitimate concern for the Black athlete at our predominately White universities it is not the central issue for poor graduation rates. If it was then our athletes would graduate in significantly higher numbers from our Historically Black Colleges and Universities (HBCU). Such is not the case. Our HBCU in Division I basketball are graduating approximately only 27 percent of its Black athletes. This places the majority share of the problem squarely within the Black community. Often we, parents and adults, only hope that the college establishment does right by our athlete. This is not a fair or even realistic expectation for the college and especially our 17-18 year old Black student, lacking confidence and maturity in every other segment of his life except for basketball. If we send academically unprepared, educationally unmotivated athletes to our HBCU and the HBCU fail to graduate them then we cannot cast blame on the White power structure. In fact we are more accountable.

It is hard to cry about the exploitation of the Black athlete on White campuses when we duplicate their results. How do you expect others to do for you when you do not do for yourself? Furthermore, while the White colleges take our most talented players, the athletes attending our HBCU are not generally pro prospects (although they still think they are) thus eliminating the excuse of leaving early for the NBA. Therefore, the athletes should have a better understanding of the value of a college degree and the HBCU should have a higher rate of graduation. Apparently, our

Black community and culture is too engrossed with athletic achievement and our athletes are too willing to unnecessarily trade educational success for the NBA dream.

To be perfectly honest, I was discouraged and stunned to see such poor graduation rates for Black athletes from our nation's 22 Division I HBCU. Having played college basketball at a White university and having formed relationships with Black college athletes that also had attended White universities over the last three decades, I had come to believe what I thought were two indisputable facts about the Black basketball athlete, and the colleges that played (Division I) basketball in our country. First, I believed the lack of Black athletes graduating was truly a result of exploitation by the White colleges in their pursuit and greed of the almighty dollar.

The second was that while our HBCU had always offered a better choice to play basketball and graduate, we, the Black athlete and Black sports community, had shunned them. We believed that both athletically and financially they could not compete with the big, White, power basketball universities in providing television exposure, facilities, competition, resources, and, most importantly the fast-track path to the NBA. But if graduation from college was the principal focus instead of hoops then surely the HBCU was the proper answer. Without hesitation I knew that at least the Black academic community was taking care of its own. After all, who would understand the value of a college education more than the Black men and women leaders, administrators, faculty, professors, and coaches at our HBCU? And who could provide a more visible role model or offer a more compelling testimony than this group of prominent Black leadership?

In trying to find out why our HBCU had graduation rates just as poor as the White colleges, Black leaders and coaches gave the same answers used by the White schools. The number one problem cited was that athletes come to campus with just the NBA vision and lack a commitment to education. However unlike the

White colleges, the HBCU say the lack of school and athletic funding is also a major problem. Yet, one HBCU head coach told me that expectation of graduation by the athletes is not a priority at many of the schools. The coach said, "From the school President on down, athletics and graduation are not always important. The top administrators are not visible to the athletes and neither are programs and measures for them to graduate."

This raises an interesting question. If HBCU Division I athletic programs are financially strapped, but their teams must continue to suffer the painful, belittling, sacrificial financial lamb blowout game defeat by a power university for a payday, endure a losing season (only 20 of 66 teams between 1998-2001 had winning records) and most importantly fail to graduate its Black players, shouldn't they reexamine their programs? Maybe even compete on the Division II level? After all, the White man's dream is not the only dream nor does it have to be our dream. Yet the pain of having my heavy heart and high expectations sink and press down on my churning stomach was such that I really didn't want to hear any question and answer dialog, roundtable discussions, reasons or explanations. Plain and simple: there are no excuses. The Black community must do a better job of emphasizing the significance of education to our youth and athletes before they go to college. In addition, our HBCU must seize the leadership role to make graduation a reality for our Black athletes when they come on campus.

* Black Self-Hate *

I have walked the eighth of a mile from our home to the elementary school playground with my eleven-year-old daughter to practice basketball. It is a very special time that allows bonding, communication, teaching and instruction between a father and a daughter who is smitten by the game (or perhaps seeking a way to get attention from a hooked on hoops dad.)

On more than one occasion, we have gone to the playground on a Saturday morning or Sunday afternoon to find half of the court covered with broken glass from a bottle of liquor. Determined to take advantage of the opportunity to practice, I painstakingly remove chunks of the jagged broken flask and shreds of glass. I take the twenty minutes to remove all the glass in case of a fall and a subsequent cut that would require stitches and a tetanus shot.

Since I have played on the playgrounds of DC for years, it is very easy for me to envision what led to the bottles smashed on the court. My neighborhood is just five minutes from the DC border and is predominately Black. More than likely, young men under the daily influence of self-hate and rage, now fueled by the intoxicating drink, argued during a basketball game. Unable to resolve their disagreement they decided in a fit of defiance to end the game for everyone involved.

* Lack of Ethnic Value *

A Black man and godfather of a highly touted high school basketball star was quoted in a national sports publication as saying, "You go up to Chicago, they [Black youth] have talent but they're out of control. You ever go into an abandoned home and turn on the lights? That's how they play in Chicago. Like roaches, scattered in all directions." How can a Black man consciously equate Black youth and their style of play in basketball to a filthy and hideous insect? Just as disgraceful as thinking it is saying it to a White reporter for publication. Clearly, this is a person devoid of ethnic pride for his own kind. How tragic it must be to look in the mirror every morning and instantly devalue yourself. Yet, the Black community is seemingly very comfortable with its own comparisons that label us below a man.

I had just officiated an All-Star game outside of Baltimore. In the gymnasium lobby after the game a coach that I had not seen in several years called to me, " Yo, dog! I saw you out there working hard." The coach, who like myself was a Black man over 45 years of age, meant nothing by the greeting nor was any offense taken. The point is that instead of a name we have found it culturally acceptable to be called "dog." Black youth address each other by "dog" or "nigga" out of habit. In my opinion, it is a negative affirmation revealing a lack of pride in yourself and your race.

* Media Stereotyping *

In the early spring of 2000, TNT cable network produced a ballyhooed documentary called "On Hallowed Ground." The presentation attempted to trace the background of the famed Rucker basketball league in New York City. What the show ultimately turned out to be was a promotion for a touring band of New York basketball players playing in various cities over the summer against similarly constructed teams. The documentary displayed Black athletes and playground basketball at its stereotypical, demeaning, and mythical worst. It was replete with Globetrotter showboating, minstrel show theatrics, tribal-like rituals, and reservation-like customs. The show depicted an inner city Black athlete that was only content jiggling and wiggling, preening and prancing on the basketball court for other worship starved Blacks watching from benches, bleachers, tops of fences and even trees.

The players, personally highlighted during the show, were talented athletically. However, they were too weak of mind and undisciplined to avoid sex, drugs, liquor, and crime and consequently their attempts to leave the "hood" and make it big were derailed. The show only reinforced the misconception that playground basketball is not winning basketball but a sideshow circus. Meanwhile, the Black athlete, because of his natural laziness, anti-social behavior, self-destructive tendencies, and apathy toward everything outside of basketball, needed the support and guidance of the nurturing White overseer.

Most Blacks I consulted about the show found it uninformative and even insulting. Whites on the other hand found it entertaining and enlightening. Then, the reasons for the difference came to me. While Black athletes, especially those from the big city, have seen, on a daily basis how life stops many basketball prodigies from besting their environment, Whites, without the up close attachment and personal relationship are constantly inquisitive and always searching for a magical answer why we dominate the sport.

Too often African Americans watch sports without a critical analysis. Sports in general and watching televised sports in particular are given a free pass regarding race. We are very content to root for the home team or alumni university and leave any unpleasant social issues on the sidelines. This inattentive and nonchalant attitude is a principal reason why sports tyrannize the Black male. African Americans watch and listen to too much sports where too many things are said by too many people (predominately White) that aren't held accountable by Black people.

* Cultural Insensitivity *

In the spring of 2001, three networks combined to televise 34 straight days of NBA playoff basketball. On many nights four and five games could easily be watched. During one midweek night game, late in the playoff series between Philadelphia and Milwaukee, NBC analyst Bill Walton, a White NBA Hall of Fame center, stated that Milwaukee guard Sam Cassell, a Black athlete from Baltimore, needed to get the "street" out of his game. Cassell was complaining to the referees about foul calls and eventually received a technical foul for his verbosity. Walton's remark was borderline racial, or at the very least culturally ignorant. I bristle when White folk take the liberty to tell Black folk what is good and bad about our culture when they do not understand our culture. And make no mistake about it, Walton's comment was about being Black and was used as a negative critique. "Street" is a sports code word for inner city or a Black style of playing the game. (When was the last time an announcer called for a player to get the "suburb" out of his game?)

The fact that Walton was criticizing Cassell's emotion as opposed to his style of play by telling him to remove the "street" from his game displays ignorance at what got Cassell to the NBA in the first place. His competitive spirit, emotion, feistiness, resiliency, and toughness in challenging every obstacle in his path, even authority if necessary to rise above his environment elevated Cassell to an elite NBA player. Talent alone may get you to the NBA, but a strong heart and willpower can keep you there. It is amazing how White society wants the Black athlete to be exciting, daring, and physically aggressive on the court yet become emotionally docile and passive off the court.

That in part may explain why Walton's partner in the telecast, Steve Jones, a Black man and former NBA player that continually has a point-counterpoint relationship with Walton during the telecasts, let Walton's comments about Cassell fall like a lead balloon. It appears it is better to tread lightly and conform than speak up about an obvious, culturally insensitive remark. Meanwhile, the subliminal message to Black youth listening is that their way of playing basketball is inadequate and that the White spectator's devaluation of the Black athlete's emotional display is acceptable.

The Black youth's devotion to basketball is a relationship unparalleled in any other culture or sport. The reasons are multiple and very complex. Some I have briefly addressed while others will be discussed throughout the book. Many conspire to funnel the Black youth into an addictive, one-sided affair with the game.

The trappings of the game are only becoming more excessive each year. The aforementioned NCAA's $6 billion, 11-year television contract, which will eventually lead to increased pressures in recruiting, cheating, and Black athletes being evaluated by productivity on the court rather than in the classroom.

Other troubling issues include: NBA players' exposure and their extravagant salaries and lifestyles, the over saturation of basketball on television, and the eagerness of adults to organize basketball leagues and tournaments for youth year round, including AAU national tournaments for players as young as nine years old. In addition, as the economic gap increases between the haves and the have-nots in our society, Black athletes will see the lottery of the NBA as the answer instead of traditional values such as higher education.

Without a proper understanding of how and why basketball is so enticing to him, the Black athlete will only become more subservient to the game. A proper understanding must start with a self-evaluation. How and why does the Black athlete come to value sports, and basketball in particular with a passion second to none? What factors in the society at large and specifically in the Black community promote his all or nothing relationship with basketball? These questions and others must be addressed if the Black athlete is ever to find the elusive balance with sports, especially basketball. In the interim, the Black athlete will continue to play basketball with an intensity and NBA-bound focus, oblivious to the turmoil swirling around him.

CHAPTER TWO:
Social Issues that Funnel Black Youth Toward Basketball

Two things Black youth learn very quickly growing up are the art of the hustle and the oversized importance and presence of sports in our community. Basketball is the sport that is king. With the fast pace of city life you must find your niche, establish your own hustle and you find it quickly to become accepted and to become "cool." Every youngster's desire in the Black community of the big city in the '60s was to be considered "cool." To be called "cool" was a stamp of approval indicating that your peers accepted you. The term in the big city labeled you as "in the know" or "streetwise." You were someone that your peers wanted to seek out for advice and leadership or just wanted to be associated with.

In the Black community, sports have always been the most recognized, and the most valued way of becoming cool and establishing your niche. Elevating your self-worth through sports has been a constant of Black youth for decades. And while there were, and still are today, several other ways to be considered "cool" none is valued as much as being a successful athlete.

Among the other ways to be considered "cool" outside of sports was being able to woo the girls. Another was the ability to dress to impress, having the latest fashions and styles of clothing. It was the combined art of dressing first class but also having multiple outfits, giving the appearance that you seemed to have a new outfit for every social occasion. Back in the '60s we called it "raggin."

Also on the "cool" meter was the ability to dance, the talent to "turn out" a party as everybody watched you perform the latest dances and musical maneuvers with your own style of grace and flair. Yet another skill considered "cool" was the ability to fight, to be able to take on all comers and stand your ground with your fists.

The last way to establish yourself as "cool" growing up in the Black community is a unique concept of Black culture known as "jonin'" or the ability to "jone." (It's interesting that I could not find where the word came from yet it has both a present and past tense.) To "jone" is to make fun of or ridicule another person or group in a give and take battle of words. I have often heard it referred to in other areas as "playin' the dozens" or "wolf tickets" or "snaps" but in Washington DC it is called "jonin'".

In the Black community it is a cultural phenomenon that is cemented into our fabric and lifestyle. In that way it is comparable to our attraction to basketball and music. "Jonin'" is a sport similar to a basketball contest but without a scoreboard, time clock or penalties. The only way a "winner" is determined is by the uproarious laughter of those listening, watching, and even participating. "Jonin'" isn't intended to be vicious, although an outsider might say otherwise. Primarily, it is an attempt to make others around you laugh and to make the participants laugh at themselves. The more creative, imaginative, spontaneous, absurd, and preposterous the joking, the better you are considered at "jonin'." In reality, "jonin'" is a mechanism by which Black folk, both young and old, laugh at themselves in order to release the tensions and stress that are part of our daily struggle. As we fight for a better day, through "jonin'" we laugh instead of cry.

These were the ways that you made it to "cool" status as a youth in the big city. For the Black male the most recognized of these was the ability to play sports. As a male growing up, if you could not find your niche in one of these six categories you were likely to be an outcast. You were subject to be beaten up or picked on verbally. Ironically, most of the categories required physical presence or athletic prowess i.e. sports, fighting, and dancing. Interestingly, what was not a high priority in being "cool" was studiousness. Being a good student was not as shunned as it seems to be today with Black youth that almost want to be stupid or carefree about grades and academic achievement. For example, during my adolescence in the '60s, good studies did not register on the cool meter either positively or negatively but was what you did because you went to school. Physical gifts and tools were the important factor. Outside of "jonin'" which was a verbal comical endeavor, you had to be physically gifted. You had to play sports, fight, or dance. Even "raggin" the latest fashions was less important simply because a lot of people didn't have the funds to dress well on a steady basis.

While, these are still the staples of being accepted as cool for youth, the consequences are stunningly different. First, the penalty for making mistakes is severe, if not deadly, for our youth today. Fights are not with fists, but often with pistols and guns. Involvement with sex and having multiple relationships can be fatal with the growth of HIV and AIDS. Basketball, too, is now far more demanding and intense. You do not play just for the fun. The pressure to excel is far greater than in the '60s.

To dress well or have the latest fashions can be a precarious situation in today's world because others will literally take the clothes off your back. Indeed it is a different day than in the '60s. But oddly enough the list remains the same. Even "jonin" today, which is still cool, can lead to anger and physical or violent confrontations. (For years one of HBO cable TV's highest rated made for TV show was "DEF Comedy Jam," a program which typify Black humor.) Of course the saddest and most devastating plague to the big city is the invasion of drugs and drug abuse into our culture.

The consequences of today's accelerated lifestyle for youth are truly sad. Our children have been stripped of their innocence and fun. I often wonder as I talk with youth how they still maintain a trusting spirit. I'm glad they do. They deserve the right to enjoy their adolescence.

A major positive change from the '60s is the fact that girls are playing sports at a level and intensity greater than ever before. Scholarship opportunities and exposure are now available for girls on almost the same level as boys. This is a huge benefit for young ladies in the Black community. With the advent of women's professional leagues such as the WNBA we will begin to see young ladies setting new goals of professional sports careers that will require college degrees for the future. Hopefully, these young women will keep sports participation in a better balance than their male counterparts.

As a youngster growing up in the '60s, I quickly and easily gravitated to playing sports and "jonin'", in order to stand out. They both came very easy to me. When I wasn't playing sports, I found it easy to make people laugh, to "jone," to cut up, and poke fun at others and myself. I had an instant and witty reply to any comment or statement. It was a very enjoyable and rewarding talent and gift. Even to this day, I circle myself with friends that can laugh and take a "slam" or "jone." I enjoy being with people who have the ability to laugh at themselves and not have an outsized ego. Laughter is truly a therapeutic medicine that makes life proceed easier. Playing sports and the ability to "jone" gave me visibility and status as a youth. It made me a cut above. I had carved a niche to stand above the day-to-day commotion. To be uniquely identified and to excel is a rewarding and valuable place to occupy. All youth search for an acceptance and identity. They have a need and desire to belong, yet be recognized for their individuality and accomplishments.

In the Black community sports is the easiest and quickest way to rise above your surroundings. Adults send messages and signals, intentional and unintentional, that convey to youth that sports achievement is a valued commodity. I remember that as an above average elementary school student; the praise that came with getting good marks was simply "good job" but the passion and clamor for how I played shortstop on the baseball diamond or broke tackles on the football field was on a noticeably grander scale. There was a detectable increase in the emotion, enthusiasm, and appreciation from family, coaches, teammates, classmates, and even teachers for athletic feats than for outstanding grades.

At home good grades were expected and accepted in my household, but I can remember my father at social gatherings or parties joyfully applauding my athletic success of pitching a complete game in a 5-2 little league victory rather than speaking about an Honor Roll report card. I was often introduced to his work associates and friends with adjectives about my athletic accomplishments instead of my school successes. "Meet my son Kevin, who scored the winning basket for his boys club team."

Schools unknowingly endorse sports over academics by paying tribute to outstanding athletic achievement versus academic success. To celebrate Honor Society students and outstanding academic achievements, many schools have an awards ceremony in the gym or auditorium during school hours. Certificates and accolades are rightfully presented to the talented academic students. Conversely, to honor its sports success the school has a season ending, catered, off campus, evening banquet complete with proper attire requirements and guest speakers from the sports community. The reasons why this happens at a school are numerous, but the overriding fact is that society as a whole has a recognized practice of celebrating athletic success over academics. It may not be intended and school principals and administrators surely do not want to place a higher value on sports over academics, but the actions taken to celebrate the success of both demonstrate otherwise. Youth see and subconsciously notice the difference and conclude that sports success and accolades have greater value.

Once Black boys get a taste of athletic accomplishment, they become aware of the kingly status given athletes in the Black community. They then contrast the experience with their invisible day-to-day existence, and it starts an all encompassing journey toward the pursuit of stardom as a professional athlete. In the meantime, the void between academic and athletic achievement begins to widen to the size of a canyon. It is a gap that is probably greater for Black youth, and in particular Black males in the big city, than in any other society. The questions then become why does our community promote the Black athlete and why does the athlete see sports as the only solution to his problems?

In this country youth are invisible. They cannot vote and they cannot invoke social change. So they are usually forgotten except as political pawns to gain votes. Youth are primarily used as a political football to gain advantage for adults' hidden agendas. Youth have to struggle to find a way to be heard. In fact, poor, Black male youth are usually never heard about except for two apparent reasons: their athletic prowess and breaking the law. This invisibility combined with the good versus bad scenario leaves a gap that most young boys will try to fill first with sports participation. But what facilitates Black males to think that these are the only two life choices?

I have found that there are four persuasive themes that accentuate Black youth's push to achieve in sports. First, is the attempt to overcome low self-esteem and the consequences of poverty. Second, is the lack of positive role models other than athletics. Third, is the influence of television. Fourth, is the perception emanating from toys to the classroom to the church that White is right.

The Black males infatuation with sports is unique to the Black community. I have lived in White neighborhoods due to the extensive travel required by my father's military commitment. I quickly saw how White youth did not encounter the same problems that I had to deal with as a Black youth. Their options are greater. Their financial resources are more plentiful. Their role models and examples of success and leadership are omnipresent. Consequently, their exposure and access is boundless.

Frankly, White youth have more confidence, privilege, resources, and role models to do whatever they please. They have the mechanisms and people in leadership roles to establish ventures in any direction of life. Being Black and poor and without visible trailblazers of leadership (in comparison to Whites) leads to uncertainty over whether certain dreams are really worth having. There will probably always be a distinct difference between being raised Black and White in our country. Along with that will be a different perception and view of what the meaning of sport is all about.

In the '60s and decades prior, there was a strong belief that success through sports was our only recourse to living the good life. It was a knee-jerk response simply because the only success we saw was primarily through Black athletes. Black youth growing up did not have or see a lot of visible, tangible options for success. Therefore, growing up our goals were very modest; get a job, go into the military or hopefully, get an outside chance at going to college. This was the path followed by most of our parents, and their life, relatively speaking, seemed okay. When combined with the invisibility of Black people in other walks of life less music and sports Black youngsters didn't dream of doing too many other things.

Outside of the sports arena our successful role models were few in number. Of course there was Martin Luther King, Thurgood Marshall, Adam Clayton Powell and others, but they were pioneers and their accomplishments were generally invisible to youth due to the lack of media representation and token teachings in the classrooms. Our most visible examples of success were athletes. To see what Muhammad Ali brought to the table through his success, style, and mannerisms was totally uplifting. Ali, a big, Black, beautiful man standing 6'4" of solid muscle could dictate conversations, rhyme in rhythm through poetry, match words and wits with the best of any White journalist or television commentator and proclaim how he was the greatest fighter of all times. That he could subsequently back up his words with his tremendous skill in the ring easily made him the greatest Black sports figure in history. His impact and presence within Black America went far beyond his athletic talent. He gave Black America prominence, pride, a voice, and a new and conquering, attitude at a time of our history when it was needed most. What Ali did for the Black race can never be duplicated and, in fact, may never ever be attempted by a Black athlete again. Today's Black athlete has found that silence pays far better than righteous indignation.

In the '60s and even earlier, our best examples of success were great athletes such as Ali, Jackie Robinson, Joe Louis and Jesse Owens. Consequently, Black male youth who were already uncertain and unsure of what viable options we had in becoming successful, got an assist from our culture which worshipped Black athletes and chose sports as our way of making it big in life.

Outside of sports, Black life was treated by White society with such invisibility and triviality that White folk did not even make an honest attempt to market and advertise their products to us in order to acquire our spending dollars. How much more invisible can Black folk be than to be told in our free enterprise system that our money is worthless or at least not worth soliciting. Commercials and advertisers did not feature Black faces, much less cater to Black issues. Even the toys we had as youths were not representative of Black concerns. If Black males wanted a GI Joe action soldier the only type on the market was a White figure. If girls wanted dolls they had to buy dolls with blond hair, white skin and blue eyes. Forget about dolls that resembled a Black woman. White dolls were the only kind sold. You either had that or you were without toys.

When we bought our food and clothing we would go to the big department stores such as Sears, Montgomery Ward or Giant Food Stores. But we knew they were not ours and that we did not own them. Sure, on occasion we would have a Black face selling or ringing up our goods at the counter, but we knew that we were going to someone that did not look like us to buy our products. From toys to the products we bought we gracefully accepted our inferior status and invisibility and purchased the products we needed.

Added to the mix was the influence of television. Despite the lack of Black actors on screen in the '60s, Black folk watched (and still do today) more television than any other race of people. In the '60s, television like the Internet today, as was still too new a medium and the depths of its impact on the culture and society were still in question. At that time, television was not under as critical an analysis as it is today.

Social Issues that Funnel Black Youth Toward Basketball

When Blacks watched television in the '60s, we saw very few Black faces. The few actors we did see did not have roles that portrayed Blacks or Black life favorably. Yet we watched intently. Sitcoms such as "Leave It to Beaver," "Father Knows Best," "Bewitched", "The Brady Bunch," "The Partridge Family," "My Three Sons," and "I Love Lucy" were all programs that were completely devoid of Black faces. Occasionally, a Black show would appear such as "Julia." Naturally the main character was without a Black male figure in her life. On "Good Times," the central character was an imbecile: a stick man figure with flapping, flailing arms, protruding lips, teeth gleaming bright smile, and a shiftless, carefree countenance representing no more than a modern day Black Al Jolson. The subtle pictures portrayed by White sitcoms were especially detrimental to the mindset of Black people because they painted a rosy picture of a wholesome family setting, father, mother, outgoing children with a big house in a nice quiet neighborhood dealing with insignificant problems of growing up that were solved jointly through communication and dialog with their parents. We would watch and compare this sitcom existence with what was going on in our lives and it gave us the impression that there was a new and better world to be had living among White folks. But in order to become a part of that world, Black people seemed to rationalize that you had to become and act White.

Black people were also invisible in the classroom. There were no Black history courses offered as part of academic studies from elementary school through high school and there definitely was not a black history month. We were pretty much excluded from the textbooks in school. History lessons of the Black man always started with slavery, failing to cover any details of our existence prior to that time. This forced Black youth to grow up learning about the accomplishments and history of the White man with only a flimsy understanding of our own history and contribution to this country except for slavery. This, in turn, led Black youth to believe in the superiority of the White man and how we should be indebted to him despite our invisible and inferior existence.

Ironically, it was a White man, Noah Webster, the writer of the first American text books for school children and the first American dictionary, that best articulated the value of having your own set of standards, schooling, and books for children. In explaining why he wrote the first American textbooks in the 1700s after America gained its freedom from England, Webster stated, "If America is to stay a free country, her children need to know how to read. They need to read what Americans write not what Englishmen write. What these children need is an American textbook." It is a philosophy that should be adopted by the Black community. Just as Webster realized American books written and taught by Americans were the best options for pride and self confidence for American children, so too should Black people rely on themselves as the best teachers for our children to learn about their history and about how to sustain independence for tomorrow.

However, of all the factors that propelled Black youth's inferiority and invisibility, the most psychologically damaging and debilitating has to be the belief that God is White. It was generally accepted without question within the Black community and Black culture that God was White. To offer a modicum of doubt was considered blasphemous. Black youth could walk into just about any home in the Black community and see a portrait of a White God hanging on the living room wall, on a dining room bureau or next to a Bible on a coffee table. Black churches would have a large portrait of a White God in the vestibule or a resemblance of a White God depicted in the stained glass windows.

Yet, we seemed oblivious to God's written word and His Ten Commandments clearly stated in the bible. In Deuteronomy 5:8, *"Thou shalt not make thee any graven image, or any likeness of any thing that is in heaven above, or that is in the earth beneath, or that is in the waters beneath the earth."* Also in John 4:24 the Bible says, *"God is Spirit: and they that worship Him must worship Him in spirit and in truth."* 1 John 4:12 says, *"No man hath seen God at any time."*

We conveniently forgot about God's word and assumed that what the White man portrayed was automatically right even as he purposely denied God's word. Furthermore, we had always been taught the superiority of the White man through theology ever since we were introduced to religion during slavery. To this day, the impact of serving a White God has stunted the Black man's attempts to develop and define a positive self-image of strength, power, and independence while alternately cementing into our subconscious the superiority of the White man.

It stands to logic that if we believe that God is White and we subsequently worship Him and trust Him for our well being, then how can we trust ourselves and certainly how can we trust our Black brother? In addition, if God is White and male, who then is the closest resemblance to Him on Earth than the White man? Therefore, we subconsciously give homage to the White man while simultaneously discrediting our own talents and gifts. Worse yet, out of religious vulnerability and confusion, many Black folk yearned to be like the White man, live next to the White man and equate their success to the White man's standards, all the while denying their natural blessings from God. In fact, many Blacks even considered the divine Creator's gifts, such as skin color and hair texture as mistakes of God. Moreover, while doubting God for His presumed mistakes, they absolutely did not find any ethnic value in other members of their race.

In the '60s and '70s as we battled inferiority and invisibility, the equivalent of the American gold rush of the 1800s descended upon the Black community. Civil rights, integration, and affirmative action sprouted new goals and opportunities for Black folks and their families. Now instead of wanting to be next to White folk, opportunities were available for this to become a reality. However, in our haste to find a new identity many Black folk under the oppression of invisibility had failed to come to an understanding of their own identity. The result of trying to take on someone else's identity without understanding the history and origin of their own identity was to leave a whole generation of Black people searching cluelessly and without ethnic value in pursuit of the alleged all-American dream. This was the beginning of the phrase used in the Black community: "forgetting where you came from."

Meanwhile, Black youth, still searching for their forum to rise above the commotion and overcome invisibility but lacking the adult leadership that was now engrossed with seizing a new frontier, played ball with an even greater passion than before. Out we went to play sports, which was still our best way to get attention in the community and achieve success in the future.

26

CHAPTER THREE:
Why Basketball Is the Game of Choice

There are so many characteristics and distinctions that advance basketball for Black youth. Basketball can be played anywhere at anytime by any number of participants from one to ten. It is convenient, cheap, and easy to access, never requiring more than a ten-minute walk in any direction in most city blocks. A goal and homemade backboard and a schoolyard, playground or recreation center can easily be found. Money or transportation is not a requirement. Gear or equipment is not an issue. Come as you are. Someone will have a ball or bring your own.

There are no physical stature limitations. The game values 5'5" guards just as much as 6'9" centers. The game is more dependent on creativity and individuality. It has artistry and beauty yet is flexible enough to allow its participants to shape and reshape its form by constantly soliciting new and creative methods of expression. The same hustle and cunning crafted on the streets has value on the basketball courts.

Through your own creativity and imagination a sense of independence, self-importance, and freedom is realized that often contrasts your whole daily existence. You take to the courts and you understand that your only limitations are those that you put on yourself through your own lack of imagination.

The rewards and the jubilation of the game—the made basket—are immediate, simple, definite, quick, and repetitive. When you contrast that with the struggles of day-to-day survival that Black youth face with invisibility, hopelessness and low self-esteem, it becomes quite clear how an escape to the neighborhood playground is necessary just to make it through the day.

The solitude and individuality of the game are unique for a team sport. Basketball is a release where you need not ask anyone for assistance. You can practice and improve your game by yourself at any time. For Black youth that grow up fast and learn to distrust most of their surroundings, basketball becomes one of the few venues that youth can call honest. You shoot at the basket and you either make it or miss it. What can be more honest than that?

There is no sport that can rival the sweet perfection of the made basket. The shot arched from afar. The orange sphere in flight with its backspin and rotation, softly hitting the back rim and dropping through the net is euphoric. The harmonious sound of nylon cord and rawhide leather as the ball nestles in the net has no comparison. This undeniable sound is often imitated but never duplicated by fans and players alike. Swish! Yet as beautiful and as harmonious, genuine and true is the made basket it is also decisive and final, oblivious to commentary, speculation, and opinion to its degree of authenticity. The ball went through the basket. Period. End of conversation. How it came to get towards the hoop can be debated, but whether it went into the basket is indisputable.

For the Black youngster the made basket is captivating and diametric to his day-to-day survival. When you sink the jumper there is no criticism, no denial, oppression or excuses. There is no long term, pie in the sky, far reaching promise of tomorrows that you are told to strive for by teachers and parents. Nope, none of that. To the contrary, the made basket is an absolute, unyielding, indisputable statement of success that can be repeated time and time again. The control and independence afforded by basketball combined with its intoxicating beauty and grace and the obliging string music of the made basket all merged with the adulation that accompanies athletic success in the big city proves to be too irresistible to deny for many Black athletes.

As a youngster, I would retreat to the playground and shoot basket after basket uninterrupted and oblivious to day-to-day occurrences. I would imitate the spin dribbles of my idol, Earl "the Pearl" Monroe. I would set up game situations—10 seconds left, at the top of key, the score 101-100, improvising a series of moves with the ball to shake my imaginary defender to get off the winning shot. And naturally, if I failed to hit the shot I was fouled and had to make two free throws to win the game. I would create this scenario time and time again indifferent to my surroundings, often ignoring the impending darkness of night. I needed no companionship nor did I seek any. Basketball is the only team sport that allows one to perfect the essence of the game, putting the ball through the basket without any support or assistance from another. In this way basketball was also a way to elevate your own self-worth. Immediately, and without having to deal with any long term commitment, faith, and promises from others.

Growing up you learn to rely on each day as it comes. Your day-to-day welfare is always first. You learn in the city, especially being raised poor and Black, that getting through the day is the goal. Goal setting and believing in the promise of a better day goes to the backburner. It is not how it should be but it is reality for most Black youth. So, when youth take to the court, basketball provides an opportunity for instant gratification that cannot be found in many other areas of daily living.

For example, teachers say to work hard and plan to go to college. But if you do not see people going to college in your community or even in your family, or you are not exposed to what college means, your interest is limited. Those that you did know that went to college were invariably athletes. They went to college through sports. Aside from teachers you did not see a lot of people going off to college then returning to their communities. Consequently, you do not strive for the goal of college because it does not seem real or possible and you question its relevance. Besides, the worry is getting through the day at hand and not a tomorrow that seems far off in the distance.

Moreover, it was easier to set immediate goals of playing basketball where you can take to the courts by yourself and reach personal athletic accomplishments. It is easy to gauge athletic development and success because they are very simple and quantifiable through basketball—make 10 or 20 free throws or jump shots in a row or make three point shots from the top of the key or the deep corner. These are tangible goals that an athlete can achieve to evaluate how he has improved from, say, Monday to Friday. From ball handling to shooting to rebounding to playing defense the game of basketball allows for so much diversity and creativity and ways to excel. To become a standout in the game you have to become proficient in more than one area of the sport. These characteristics helped create my passion for the game so much so that individual practice was always enjoyable and obligatory. I was of the belief that a day that I did not practice was a day that somebody else was getting better than me.

Physically, the game requires brute strength yet finesse. It requires will-o'-the wisp quickness and a lithe frame but also an ability to anchor and hold your ground. All of these attributes swept me up in a wave of passion and commitment for the game that can only be defined as an addiction. Basketball has obvious parallels to city living,–its raw emotion and quick pace and its definite and immediate give and take. This, combined with its visual beauty and the requirements of an active imagination over physical stature, has proven to be a sports elixir to Black athletes.

Basketball's hold on the Black community is mind-boggling. Growing up as a male youth you cannot escape the game. It is as if the game is handed down from generation to generation like a family heirloom. Black folks play basketball gleefully. Even if the game were not viewed as our only escape out of our environment, we would still play basketball for pleasure. Basketball is a huge part of the Black culture. Similar to our professed gift for music or to traditional foods that are supposed delicacies of Black culture (such as our misguided affinity for pork and pig parts that our ancestors were forced to eat during slavery), basketball fits right into the spectrum of the Black life style. It is not questioned, it just happens. It is a sports rite of passage, a Black tradition that only feeds and fosters our addiction toward the game.

Why Basketball Is the Game of Choice

Clearly, and without hesitation, there is no other sport that captivates a race of people as passionately as basketball does the Black community. There are several criteria to support the statement:

It is fast paced and aggressive. Unlike football, which is played in an open field with shining uniforms that resemble a suit of armor, basketball is played without protective gear and with minimal attire in a confined area resembling city dwellings. The game is played with an emphasis on man-to-man and one-on-one confrontation. Yet, unlike boxing, basketball has far more creativity, flair, and artistry combined with team principles and continuity. Basketball offers a dream of a position on the floor for every man regardless of size and stature. This reinforces to youth the hope that they can conquer their surroundings. Anyone who has ever made a basket can envision themselves as the star of the team filling the hoop with shot after shot.

The game itself is enveloped with emotion and its answers are decisive and immediate. When you play the game of basketball there is no hiding. You play to win. You put your game on display against the next man and either you can play or you are beaten. It is parallel to life in that you take care of business or you are placed at a disadvantage. Another similarity to life on the streets is the pace of the game–quick, frenetic, sudden, intense, and raw yet allowing artistry, creativity, imagination, and individuality.

But clearly the most defining characteristic to why basketball is king is the element of one-on-one confrontation. No other team sport allows one person of any size to display so many varied and multiple ways to determine the outcome of winning and losing than in the game of basketball. From the 5'5" guard with crafty ball handling and outside shooting to the 6'6" forward with versatility and athleticism and marksmanship to the 7' center with his inside presence, rebounding and shot blocking all are capable of dominating a basketball game.

One-On-One Basketball

It is the one-on-one feature of the game that allows every man to not only participate, but also rise above the commotion and individually excel, that appeals so strongly to the Black athlete. Basketball especially through one-on-one allows the Black male, to shed his faceless and invisible emptiness and, through his own imagination and creativity generate, a positive impact. One-on-one basketball affords a control that the Black youth generally does not have in any other facet of his life. One-on-one gives the Black athlete expression, freedom, power, individuality, and purpose, all of which are in short supply being raised in the Black community.

In addition, notoriety and reputations are created through the sports community's craving and acceptance of one-on-one play. Its intrigue goes well beyond who won the game but includes which players were "taken to school" and victimized one-on-one. Often, spectators sitting in close quarters to the scantily dressed players with muscles, emotions, and thoughts exposed for all to judge are enthralled by which players won the one-on-one confrontations just as much as the victory. Many times, the question that is asked after who won is an inquiry as to how many points the star players scored.

The one-on-one aspect is valued more in the Black community because trust is not given up easily. It becomes a badge of courage, a badge of honor. Youth grow up in the city suspicious and leery at all times. In particular, you learn to distrust what you see in society and the mechanisms that are supposedly in place to help, such as law enforcement and government. In the city you learn to take care of your own business and to be careful in whom you trust. Basketball more than any other team sport allows you to be within a team setting, but to have a major impact on the game through one-on-one confrontation or a reliance on your own individual skills to have a major impact on the game. This is a large benefit leading to the attraction to the game for the Black athlete. You play the game and can control it through your own resources. If you have the skill level, the one-on-one talent you can lift your team to success while playing in a team framework. Thus, youth in the big city take to the playground with a mindset that the game can be played without even trusting your teammates if necessary.

A Black athlete can play basketball with the knowledge that he can control his fate in the game through his one-on-one capabilities. He doesn't have to rely on anybody else including his possibly faint-hearted or less committed teammates. Therefore, he will not and cannot be let down or disappointed as he has been by so many others throughout his life. Through his one-on-one gifts he has control. One-on-one basketball is born of the Black athlete's distrust and suspicions of his environment. So, when Black athletes play one-on-one and become proficient stars through this ability it is a reaction to being raised in the fast, impersonal environment of the Black community where you have to learn quickly to trust your own instincts for your survival and safety each day.

That is one of the attractions that brought me to the game of basketball. The mere fact that I could play the game without the aid of anybody else was special. I could play of my own will, with my own imagination and my own time frame. I could improve and excel at the game without the resources of anybody else. I did not need anybody to pitch to me, run pass patterns or quarterback and pass to me. All I needed was a ball and a rim. I didn't have to trust or depend on anyone or allow anyone to disappoint me because of their other commitments or situations. I could not be hurt by anyone because I did not need anyone.

This attitude of individuality and refusal to become dependent on anybody sets the tone of how basketball played by the Black athlete is different than that of the White ballplayer. Because of the Black athletes, fast paced, distrusting, suspicious, hurtful upbringing, Black youth take these same emotions and thoughts to the court and play the game the same way. Black athletes learn to rely on their own instincts to beat an opponent, to score and ultimately to win. The same abilities and instincts used to hustle and exist on the streets are brought to the courts and the athlete becomes proficient as a one-on-one player. For many Black players one-on-one is a reflective self-defense mechanism; suit of armor to shield them from being constantly hurt and disappointed by others on the court the way they have been victimized off the court. Still, for other Black players, one-on-one basketball is the escape and release from their apathetic and invisible existence. It is a solo act to express their independence and individuality while commanding respect and power in an otherwise powerless and forgotten reality.

Conversely, in the White community the White athlete has a much more trusting, giving and compassionate upbringing and you can see that manifested on the basketball courts. The so-called "White game" is one of picks and screens with a reliance and dependence on his teammates. Teamwork is expected, accepted, and trusted. The upbringing of the White athlete is more social, outgoing, and neighborly. Having been afforded more exposure and fewer setbacks he has higher expectations of success for himself and from others such as his coach and teammates. The White athlete has a healthy regard for authority and having never been betrayed by leadership, is more inclined to trust and receive coaching. Consequently, the White athlete's style of basketball is clearly different than that of the Black athlete. What the Black and White athletes bring to the court from their backgrounds is instrumental in the roles they acquire on the courts.

Black players are not raised with the same trust. They want to have it and they want to be trusting but situations always seem to conspire to betray their attempts to reach out to others. Coolidge High School in northwest Washington DC hired a new football coach. The young Black man had played football for a recognized top 20-college program. He had previous high school assistant coaching experience from the well funded, community supported programs in affluent Fairfax County in the suburbs of northern Virginia. What he did not have was a background in working with youth from a rough area in a financially strapped school and athletic system. Midway through the season the coach simply disappeared. Much of the equipment also was missing. There was no explanation to the young athletes. What did remain was a permanent scar on the hearts of the Black young men that had begun to trust in authority and leadership. This type of scenario re-enforces why Black players often believe that if it is to get done athletically or in a game situation they will have to do it themselves, similar to the environment lived off the court. Experience can be a hard teacher for Black youth. This, in part, defines a large reason for the difference between White and Black players style of play. It has less to do with the physical gifts of a player but more so with the mental makeup that is brought to the game.

Thus, the consensus among Black youth was that White players that usually do not live in the community could not play the game on a level comparable with Black athletes. Our pride and athletic arrogance would preclude us from believing that the game of basketball could be played better or at a higher level by anyone else. Today, most Black athletes without hesitation will say they are better players than White athletes. My high school teammates and I were quite secure in our knowledge that we were instantly better than White players. Not only did we believe we were better skilled ballplayers, but we were stronger of heart and mind and we could easily intimidate White athletes because they would be afraid to compete. Many of my teammates strongly held this belief yet because of their upbringing some had never played against or with White players. For my high school teammates, the question became where did the assumption that they were superior to White basketball players come from?

One answer had to be the belief that living in the Black community makes one automatically mentally and physically tougher than in an environment where you have all the luxuries of life. A second answer would be the visual presentation from watching television. Sports programming was on the fast track in the late '60s and '70s and its popularity and hold, especially on Blacks, was tremendous. As we watched, we invariably saw Black basketball players having huge success at the expense of White players. Nowhere on television this side of soul music could you see Blacks on television exceeding the efforts of White folks. When you mesh the reasons why Black youth play the game, and then add the significant success of large numbers of Black athletes playing the game in college and the professional ranks, it becomes very easy to see how basketball takes off from being an attraction to an addiction for Black athletes. Despite all the injustices and putdowns and invisibility that Black youth have encountered they have always held outstanding basketball players in high praise. Another answer was word of mouth from Black athletes that played college ball in other parts of the country and after returning home relayed the message that the Black athlete was better but never got the proverbial "breaks" or fit the system to become the star.

The belief that the Black athlete is a superior player to Whites is not borne exclusively of a racial stereotype or a social class prejudice. In fact, its deepest origin is probably rooted in an opposition to the style of play of the White athlete. Each athlete brings to the game of basketball a different set of goals, objectives, and reasons for playing. This is what augments the Black athlete's rationale that he is a better player than the White athlete. It is the Black athlete's disrespect of the style of play of the White athlete that is the issue. The Black athlete believes the game as played by White athletes is soft, methodical, slow, boring and lacking spontaneity, flair, emotion, and showmanship—a style unacceptable and insulting to the so-called city game. Conversely, Whites look at the game as exhibited by Black athletes and say it is undisciplined, lacking fundamentals and played in an out of control manner.

Why Basketball Is the Game of Choice

For many Black athletes life is fast paced, always changing and challenging, and always confrontational. Nothing is given. Consequently when the Black youth takes to the basketball court his style of play is synonymous to his off the court lifestyle. His game is played in a frenetic pace but with a purpose. His game features an emphasis on one-on-one play because of his off the court pain from trusting others and learned value of self-reliance. His game is played with flair, bravado, and showmanship because of his off the court struggles for visibility and accomplishment. His game is played with intimidation and physical play because he learned off the court that nothing is given to him and that which he has acquired can be stripped away in the blink of an eye. His game is played with emotion because through his lack of exposure and opportunity off the court he believes sport, is his only sanctuary. It can provide peace, instant gratification, hope, and a better way of living.

By contrast, the White athlete who is raised in a totally different environment plays the game of basketball with different expectations and standards of success. He plays a more dependent and team oriented game because he has witnessed off the court how status, financial wherewithal, trusting his neighbor, community involvement, and White privilege has brought about promises and creature comforts in life. The pace of the White player is slower because he has an understanding of patience and authority. For example, when the coach tells a player that he will have an open jump shot once he comes around a double screen, he trusts that this will happen. He will believe that the screens will be set by his teammates and the ball will be passed in time, for him to shoot the ball. His off the court accomplishments and surrounding support system of family and community gives him the patience and confidence to believe that good results will occur.

However his game lacks creativity primarily because off the court White privilege has brought success easy and without a price to pay and he has never known hunger and denial. He has not had to be resourceful and definitely does not comprehend the hustle of the streets. His game does not include intangibles such as physical and verbal intimidation. Victory is solely determined by the team with the most points on the scoreboard. This is because the rules of the game, as are those off the court, are determined and structured for White society's best interest and those that have financial wealth. His game is played expressionless, at least in comparison to the Black athlete, because off the court he has been exposed to options, and different pathways to success. Basketball is not an all or nothing proposition. In fact, it is often just a form of recreation. He understands that he can walk away from the game at any time and his identity and chances for success will remain intact.

The Black athlete plays the game of basketball with a resolve, force, and unreserved passion unmatched by any other race in any other sport. The frightening point is that without proper life changing options and alternatives the game will only cause pain once the ball stops bouncing and the nets are cut down.

* Feeding the Habit–Television *

If you look at when the Black explosion and domination of sports came about it is easy to see the correlation with the boom of television in the '60s. Prior to that time, Black success in sports was taking place but generally not at a pace that upset or concerned White society. Certainly, Black success in sports was not dominant enough in the '60s to have White society question itself as to whether they were indeed the inferior athletes, which takes place frequently today. In all probability, the only reason why Black domination in football and basketball did not take place sooner was segregation and exclusionary practices that denied the Black athlete opportunities to play these sports at the college and professional levels.

As basketball became more and more a priority and concentration for Black athletes, television was yet another wave of influence that accentuated his addiction and the belief that the sport was his salvation. Clearly the media, with television's portrayal of Black life in general and especially its depiction of Black athletes, help amplify the notion that Black athletes are superior to the White player. Oddly enough, I do not think this was the intention of sports and television but, nonetheless, it helped feed the proposition that the Black athlete was the best, especially in basketball. The '60s were a time when Black youth had few visible role models in other professional venues; marketers and advertisers generally did not cater to us. We were not visible in the history books or in the classrooms. Yet the one medium where the Black community could see people like themselves having success, and particularly success against the White establishment, was in sports on television. That was a dynamic that even the White dominated media failed to see how much of a booster shot it was to the self esteem of Black folk. Watching successful Black athletes heightened the Black community's thirst to play sports.

Yet there was an important trade-off as the Black athlete gained an all around self-confidence. An attitude was established that if the Black athlete didn't make it in basketball he could still make it successfully in life. The added confidence said to the Black athlete that he could be anything he wanted to pursue. After being downtrodden and denied, neglected and rendered invisible by White society, Black youth now saw how they not only could compete but defeat the White player in sports. It created a sense of confidence that not only could we succeed in sports but also that we could succeed in other walks of life, especially in coordination with the liberation provided by the Civil Rights movement. For Black boys growing up in the big city in the '60s without tangible goals and with low self esteem running rampant, watching Black athletic success was a combustible fuel to jump start the engine of our imaginations and dreams and actions. All of the sudden what teachers and parents told youth about education had merit. The pieces, of the puzzle were now taking shape. The thought process became, 'yes I can see it happen on basketball courts and football fields so why couldn't it happen in the classrooms or the boardrooms?' All of a sudden, sports and academics became an easier vision and an understanding of how they could co-exist ensued.

To heighten the awareness that we are good athletes, and that the Black man can become a champion we would also listen to how commentators and sportscasters would heap acclaim and praise on the accomplishments of the Black athlete. With each success story of a thirty-point outburst by Oscar Robertson, or 40-50 point game from Wilt Chamberlain and other athletes, we would immediately go to the courts with an unabashed desire to be like these athletes. We would watch and listen intently and marvel as these athletes were described with descriptive adjectives and phases such as "natural athlete," "God-given ability," "quick," "gifted player," "strong and powerful," "explosive," "great jumping ability." Granted, although we were never described with adjectives highlighting intelligence, it did not matter at the time. Just the fact that we were having success and becoming winners and champions over Whites and we were commended for doing it with increasing frequency by predominately White commentators was exciting. To listen as Black athletes were complimented by White commentators and sportscasters as if they were naturally superior because God made them that way only facilitated our belief that nobody could play the game of basketball better than the Black athlete. The belief became for the Black athlete that sports, and in particular basketball, was our undeniable and destined course in life.

Basketball was taking off in the '60s and early '70s as a spectator sport and the White media probably didn't comprehend just how much of a stimulus it would be to the Black community to see Black athletes succeed. Perhaps they were too engrossed with the popularity of the sport and the windfall of profits to really take a hard look at its impact on Black society. In the '60s, there were just

Why Basketball Is the Game of Choice

three major networks. This was before the NCAA phenomenon called March Madness. This was before "Magic" Johnson and Larry Bird took college and professional basketball to another level of participation and viewership. This was before cable television and 60-plus channels of programming. Basketball was becoming bigger and bigger in popularity and in its haste to get in on the ground floor and ride the rocket of financial success, the White dominated media did not realize the energy lift provided to the Black community by watching so many Black athletes succeed.

On the other hand, perhaps the media did not care if Black folk celebrated and enhanced their self-respect through sports. They needed the style, flair, and athletic labor provided by the Black athlete to sell the game. I believe the prevailing attitude was "keep the dunks right on coming, all the way to the bank." Meanwhile, through our own addiction to hoops, the Black community was more than willing to oblige and continue to entertain. Basketball, which already had an overblown and distorted value in the Black community was now front and center in the community through its popularity on television.

* Parents Missing in Action *

As Black athletes become more and more committed to the game of basketball the one constant needed to keep the game in perspective is the direction of concerned parents. Unfortunately, parental and adult participation in the athletic careers of their children has always been glaring by its absence. As I travel from gym to gym and referee high school basketball games from financially strapped southeast Washington DC to the affluent suburbs of Columbia, Maryland, the lack of parental involvement for Black youth is very noticeable.

When I work games in the surrounding suburbs of Washington DC, including predominately White Montgomery and Howard counties, there is greater participation among White parents concerned about the athletic progress of their sons and daughters. When I officiate the games of the private schools, the parents both, Black and White, that are paying huge tuitions for their child to attend the schools also seem to be actively involved in their athletic pursuits. Yet, when I officiate games within the Washington DC city limits adult participation is comprised of the school administrators and school faculty, and their numbers far outdistance those of the parents in the stands.

The problem is so grim in Washington DC public schools that "Mac" Brown, the athletic director and head varsity women's coach at Coolidge High School in northwest Washington DC, told me his girls team was booed at the free throw line by the fans from a visiting suburban team. The opposing team had triple the support and attendance in the stands during a home game. Brown estimates that in his 16 years of coaching in the Washington DC School system less than 15 percent of the parents participated in their children's athletic careers. Yet, neighboring Howard County, an affluent and racially diverse community approximately 45 minutes from the Washington DC border, has its games starting at 5:00 pm for boys and girls varsity with a junior varsity contest starting at 3:30. Even with the early starting times the games are well supported by parents. Having officiated games for years in Howard County, I alternately admire their parental support and anguish over the lack of involvement of Black parents.

One experience best illustrates the stark contrast between parental involvement of suburban Howard County, and that of its big city brother Washington DC. Spingarn High School located in northeast Washington would become city basketball champions in 2000. Late in the season, the Green Wave played rival H.D. Woodson High, about a 10-minute ride from the Spingarn campus. The game was an anticipated, hotly contested affair between neighborhood rivals with Spingarn rated the number one team in the area. Indeed, the atmosphere within the gym could be called unsettling. First, the

Why Basketball Is the Game of Choice

Spingarn spectators, clusters of leering Black males, had carried an intimidating aura about them throughout the year. Many of their supporters would come to the games in groups of six to ten, complete with bandanas, dark shades and heavy coats, the prerequisite attire of toughness in the big city. They would posture, stare and assemble in the doorways. Their presence often intimidated the other team even when Spingarn was the visiting team!

Because the Woodson High School students and athletes knew many of the Spingarn crowd they were not fearful. Meanwhile, as the stands continued to fill before the game, the marijuana stench permeated the gymnasium as fans came into the gym immediately after getting high in the parking lot or their cars. Profanity seemed to be the only language spoken. The police on location probably could have arrested a third of the spectators for drug violations but seemed reluctant to intercede as long as things remained peaceful. The aura of the evening clearly portrayed that the event was not a family outing, especially for young children. With the mostly teenage and young adult local neighborhood crowd in attendance, outsiders from other environments such as the suburbs would feel very uncomfortable, to say the least. However, to the basketball player and fan this atmosphere is equivalent to the Final Four. Raw, intense, menacing and confrontational, are characteristic of big city basketball on the court and many times in the stands. Fortunately, except for a couple of verbal confrontations leading to posturing and threats which police immediately terminated, the game was played without disruption.

Interestingly, by comparison, a good and valued friend Joseph Bross, a Jewish man and president of his own company, invited me to attend his sons' high school basketball game at Centennial High School in Columbia. The spacious school located among rolling hills, tree lined parks, and beautiful homes gives the appearance of a New England private boarding school. His sons, Scott and Josh, were on the team. Scott was the starting point guard while Josh was a shooting guard coming off the bench. I had known both teens since they were youngsters.

I was astounded at the amount of parents present for an early evening game. Not only was one parent in attendance, but for some of the athletes both mother and father were present. The game was a mid-week, 5:00 pm start—requiring most parents to leave work early. The parents exchanged greetings and congratulated each other on the team's victory in the last game and the contributions of their sons on the team. The parents networked, spoke of community issues, set agendas for future games, and cheered the efforts of the Centennial athletes.

Watching the evening unfold was a pleasure and I can only equate the experience to a mini tail-gate party before a University of Maryland or, for that matter, a Washington Redskins football game; The kinship and camaraderie was that special. While the caliber of play and the intensity of the game was noticeably weaker than at H.D. Woodson High School in northeast Washington DC, the other obvious occurrence was the lack of parents at one site compared to the highly visible presence of parents at the other.

As I drove the 50 minutes home from the game in Columbia that evening, I had a myriad of emotions. I was so impressed with the dedication and devotion of the parents to the athletic progress of their sons. I wondered if the athletes knew just how fortunate they were to have caring parents that would sacrifice their time to support them. In the Black community, it seems that time is always the last thing parents are willing or able to give their children. I wondered just how much having their parents in attendance lifted the confidence and self-esteem of the athletes. I did know that having their parents at the game gave the players a perspective that basketball is just a sport and that their identity or self-worth was not tied to the outcome of the game.

Black athletes seek answers to many of the confusing questions in their lives through success on the basketball courts

Why Basketball Is the Game of Choice

because of the overemphasis of sports in the Black community. When Black parents forfeit their participation in the athletic progress of their youth, the young athletes continue their confounding relationship with basketball. Young Black athletes equate their parents' absenteeism as an endorsement that their attraction to the game, its magnified importance to their lives, and their solitary obsession with getting to the pros is indeed okay and a worthy pursuit. Consequently, their overblown and unrealistic dreams and their inflated opinion of their athletic skills keep many Black athletes on a runaway train–a professional career heading full bore toward a collision with hard core reality and statistics. I ache wishing that Black parents realize the value of giving time to their athletes instead of giving their athletes to the game so they can keep their time.

I was overly sensitive to the lack of parental and adult presence at public high school games in Washington DC as soon as I started officiating high school games during my fourth year as a referee. I even had informal and casual discussions as to why this was the case. Was it my imagination? Had parental participation at high school games always been poor? Was I just oblivious to it because I was a high school player at St. Anthony's High where because my parents paid tuition, I took their attendance at my games for granted. Regardless, now, I clearly see that parental and adult presence is lacking at the high school games of Black youth and I wanted to know why. After witnessing the game with the Bross family at Centennial High it merely reconfirmed what I already knew–Black parents and Black youth are simultaneously losing an opportunity to share, bond, communicate, educate, and mature together through the pursuit of athletic achievement. The alternative is the continuation of Black youth becoming more committed and deeply enamored to basketball as their only source of happiness and achievement rather than the game being a resource to success and fulfillment.

Understandably, there are multiple and very complex reasons as to why Black parents do not support their youth particularly on

45

the high school level. As I have spoken with teachers, administrators, coaches, and parents of athletes on this issue over the last decade, certain denominators top the list of why Black parents and adults do not attend high school games.

* **Economics.** Black families are not proprietors of their own businesses. Often they are not in management. They frequently are mid-management, clerical support, and labor personnel. Many Black parents work more than one job just to continue to stay financially afloat. The struggle to meet the material demands of every day living extends throughout the day and forces many parents to constantly battle with the allocation of their time.

They have to work odd hours or shift work. Consequently, while a 7:00 pm start for most games in Washington DC seems conducive to allowing parental involvement it is not all-inclusive. Working in a support or hourly employee capacity often does not permit a parent to arbitrarily decide when they can leave the job to attend a high school game. Having to use annual leave can result in less income later on the paycheck. Also, single families do not have their own transportation. Taking public transportation to and from games can be time consuming and very costly to families with little discretionary income. One coach of a Prince George's County school just outside the city limits said that only one of his 14 players lived in a house. Most of the athletes were from apartments. This was a typical occurrence each season.

* **Broken homes.** One parent usually the mother, heads many Black families. These families have younger brothers and sisters that require their share of attention–discipline and

46

foremost love and caring. There isn't a lot of time left in a day for a single parent to attend a weeknight basketball game. If the guardian is a grandparent, oftentimes, they simply do not have the energy to keep pace with all the activities of a teenager.

* **Young parents dealing with life and children.** A majority of the coaches I spoke with list this as the primary reason. Yet as J.R. ,Etheridge, a high school and youth league coach told me, "It may be the critical reason. But it is still inexcusable for parents that can see the pleasure and enjoyment that their child receives from sports to not participate in this endeavor from little league through high school." Nonetheless, many young parents are still searching for the answers to their own questions in life while struggling with growing children. An assistant coach at a D.C. public school asked me if I understood just how disconcerting it was for a 17- or 18- year-old young man to come home at night from a game or practice and see his 33-year-old mother dressed in a skin-tight outfit leaving for a party or club. These young adults between the ages of 27 and 35 with teenagers find that raising children and realizing their own dreams and aspirations is a very difficult challenge.

* **A neighborhood is not a community.** People keep to themselves. Families move in and out of neighborhoods more frequently for a multitude of reasons. Consequently, people don't want to get involved. Throw into the mix the fact that Black neighborhoods are not self-contained. They lack resources to grow from a neighborhood into a community and folks have to go elsewhere to spend their money for goods and services. The same scenario affects the education of their kids. In Washington DC many students attend public schools outside of their natural geographical

boundaries for various reasons. Certain schools may offer a different academic curriculum or classes, a fact which allows students to travel to different schools across town. Of course, academics are often used as a smoke-screen to allow talented athletes to move from school to school. In Prince George's County busing is in effect for many neighborhoods and schools. Camaraderie and school and neighborhood spirit are replaced with a mad dash to yellow buses with the 3:00pm dismissed bell.

The local high school is perceived not so much as belonging to the neighborhood as it is a building that houses students. The end result is that a sense of community is lost.

Oxon Hill High School in Temple Hills and Central High in Capital Heights, Prince George's County schools just outside the Washington DC border, have outstanding adult participation at their basketball games. As an official I enjoy my games at these gyms which are usually jam-packed with well-behaved enthusiastic crowds. Oxon Hill men's varsity basketball coach Billy Lanier feels that the two schools and a few others in the county have a good adult presence at games because of the stability of the surrounding neighborhoods, the year-to-year success of their programs (Oxon Hill and Central have won Maryland state championships). In addition, the high school, itself, solicits the participation of the community and has activities and programs at the school.

* **Fear.** Many adults are afraid to attend neighborhood high school games because they believe that it is unsafe getting to and from the game at night. They are concerned about their safety in the parking lots, in the stands, and after the games. When told this by a community leader working with at-risk youth I naturally asked, "Why would these parents allow their children to play ball at the same

school? If it's unsafe for the parent how can it be safe for the youth?" His reply was that the parents believe the kids know better whom they can and cannot trust. They are at the game and they are the athletes on the court. Getting to and from the game is an entirely different situation, the parents will tell you. Still disbelieving this assessment I asked, "Where does this come from? I've worked games as a referee for over 16 years and never had a problem. And naturally as the ref, I'm one of the least liked people in the gym." "True", he responded, "but you are still on the court. A lot of people, adults, and parents are lazy and make a judgment on what they watch and listen to in the news and read in the paper. They don't care to know the community and don't trust their neighborhood and can find the experience intimidating."

Probably the single biggest reason why Black parents do not actively support and monitor the athletic progress of their children is that they are too trusting of the sport and the adults that provide leadership. The prevailing attitude is that if it's sports related then it's okay. Sports, and basketball in particular, is afforded absolute respect and trust. Basketball has an unconditional grade-A standing in the Black community. Black parents feel totally safe knowing that their children are involved with sports, especially basketball. In fact some parents take basketball to an extreme and let the youth coach raise the child.

A youth league coach says that he has had kids as young as 10 years old that could stay with him the entire weekend and not once phone their parents to let them know their whereabouts. There is a false confidence among some parents in the big city that only positives can surface from participation in sports. Deriving a comfort zone with this rationalization, parents easily move onto other endeavors without concern. It is ironic that many of the same Black parents in the Black community that have a distrust for police (they are tools of the White man to corral and contain us); banks (refusing to open checking and saving accounts and rather keep their money in their homes under mattresses or in shoeboxes); Black professionals (White doctors or White accountants know more, i.e. "get me a good Jewish accountant to handle my taxes"); and each other ("don't ask me nothing, I didn't see or hear anything") have no reservations at all about turning their most precious commodity—their youngster—over to basketball.

Parents are all too trusting of the sport. It is one of the few areas (school is another) of Black culture where Black folks trust the system to care for our youth. They believe sports are the answer. It is the light for a better way in the present and the salvation for the future. The implication is that because it is basketball the best interest of the athlete will occur. This, however, is a shortsighted, selfish, and careless assessment. In today's excessive preoccupation with sports, for parents to give up involvement in their youth's athletic participation and progress can be equivalent to placing a goldfish in a piranha tank; it can be that detrimental to the thoughts and maturation process of our Black youth.

My philosophy is that our Black boys and girls are princes and princesses and can become future kings and queens. Those Black youth that have magnified their athletic talents to play sports at a high and proficient level have the opportunity to provide tremendous leadership and exact positive change for themselves, their family, and their community. This however, must come through education, awareness, direction, and a perspective that can only be truly provided by parents and guardians.

CHAPTER FOUR:
How Basketball Is Played in the Black Community

In the Black community basketball is played with physicality, emotion, flair, and intimidation from elementary school to college. The game as played by Black athletes in most Black communities is clearly a manifestation of the sudden, rough, lifestyle learned in crowded, untrusting urban neighborhoods. Victory in basketball is taken never just won. In addition, the victory is often more than just a final score, it is a style. Victory in basketball entails personal pride and the establishment of turf in one-on-one personal confrontation.

Intimidation is a huge part of basketball. It is the testing of a competitor's heart and desire by any way possible if it will help to win the game. Intimidation in the big city is considered fair play. In basketball there is a thin line between the code of the streets and the way the game is played. The same attitude of the street hustle, of doing whatever it takes to get by, is the same disposition brought to the court.

The Black athlete believes that society's laws are unfair and stacked against him. These laws are designed specifically to protect, serve, and better the interest of the privileged White and wealthy of this country. The Black athlete has to look no further than his own downtrodden, apathetic neighborhoods. Consequently, when the Black athlete plays basketball he has no hesitation about deviating from the rules of the game.

Every player knows, or will come to know, that in city basketball the rules of the game and society's laws are secondary to the code of conduct on the street. The code of the street, for example, says if you take me to the hoop I, in turn, take you. If you hit me with an elbow I hit you with an elbow. Players do not look for coaches, referees or teammates for assistance. The athletes play the game to exact their own justice.

51

The implication is not that the Black athlete plays the game in a lawless, vigilanti-like manner disrespectful of the game. Absolutely not. The Black athlete's style of playing the game has been tweaked and modified to make it more conducive and compatible to the lifestyle lived off the court by its participants. It is a temperament that says you take care of your own business and do not rely on anyone else (government, police, coaches, teachers, even parents) for support. The Black athlete is respectful of the rules of the game, but certain codes of the "streets" often extend beyond many of the sport's regulations. The rules are acknowledged and accepted but only with the same regard that one has for posted speed limit signs on the roadways. You see the city or state speed limit but you adhere to it or exceed the required speed based on your own value of time, safety, and, most importantly, the presence of the police.

Basketball in the Black community has four distinct components: Physical play, intimidation, emotion, and flair. Clearly the most profound staple of the game is intimidation. Physical play, emotion and flair are necessary to play the game and are examples of how the game is played differently than anywhere else but the one element that separates the game apart from others is the use of intimidation. Physical play, emotion, and flair are how the game is played; intimidation is how the game is won.

* Physical Play *

Physical play is a large part of Black basketball. You are clearly defined as having heart or you are labeled as "soft" on how you react to physical play. In 20 years of playing basketball on the playgrounds, very rarely have I heard a player call a foul for what the rulebook would call off the ball contact, rebounding, post play where players establish a position close to the basket to receive a pass or pursue a loose ball. I have never seen an offensive foul or charge taken in a playground game.

How Basketball Is Played in the Black Community

I can remember participating in a playground game while on defense when I was bowled over by the offensive player with the ball. The player then proceeded to dribble around my outsprawled body and sink an uncontested jumper. A teammate came over to me and calmly stated, "Any time a player hits you like that, take him down to the floor with you." It wasn't a criticism, it was just an illustration of the code of play on the playground. There aren't any charges or offensive fouls on the playgrounds so if a collision happens, then take the player down so you will not give up an easy basket. No questions asked. You dare not call "foul" for any of these calls or you will be labeled soft. Physical play is accepted and you continue to play the game. The overriding principle in Black basketball is that victory is taken, not won.

The most vivid illustration of physical play is "game point." This is when two teams are tied and the next basket determines the winner. The victor will remain on the court to play again and the losers must leave the court, usually resulting in a lengthy wait, perhaps as long as a couple of hours, to play again. The pursuant physical contact to score and defend can be brutal and intense, yet it is anticipated and culturally accepted as playground basketball. The underlying premise understood among the players is that the team with the strongest willpower and desire to win will ultimately decide the outcome.

* Emotion *

The Black athlete comes to the basketball court with a wide variety of emotions. Heading the list among those emotions is the belief that basketball is his salvation. Basketball is his pride. Basketball is his refuge. Basketball is where he can proclaim to his whole world that he is somebody, that he is not invisible. He can stand tall and can accomplish. With this demeanor, Black youth take to the courts.

There are multitudes of emotions that are pent up and subsequently surface and are released through basketball. This occurs not just through the physical endeavors of running, jumping, and shooting. These are athletic releases. Emotions are released by the pride and sense of accomplishment gained through playing basketball. Of the collage of emotions brought from the environment to the court by the Black athlete, the strongest is the desire to be seen, and acknowledged. Basketball becomes the Black athlete's forum to be recognized and to have pride and success in achieving. Basketball becomes a way to communicate and express himself while standing tall among the apathy and invisibility that surrounds his daily life. Therefore, with all these emotions tied to his success on a basketball court, the Black athlete plays the game in a very volatile, prideful, aggressive, and confrontational manner. This attitude scares a lot of people, especially the White power structure which has legislated ways to banish the display of emotion from the game. Nevertheless, this same emotion attracts the fans to television sets and arenas in record numbers across the country.

In order to rebel against invisibility in his life, the Black male has always sought attention on and off the court. In our dress, we set the fashion trends for this country. We are the biggest consumers of sports merchandise. Marketers will tell you that the Black community is targeted for new products and trends because we are a willing and gullible consumer. The reason why the Black community, and primarily Black youth, are the number one consumers is the alleged self worth that is derived from wearing brand name clothing and athletic apparel. We are often so defeated, and consumed with self-hate that instead of looking inward we reach out to another culture to provide us with value, even if that value is nothing more than wearing a sweatshirt or a pair of sneakers. Our lack of self worth, personal pride, and ethnic value is so rampant and pervasive that they are the impetus and starting point for many of the social ills that plague the Black community.

When we do reach a level of success, our first substantive job for example, the first thing that young Black males do is buy a

How Basketball Is Played in the Black Community

flashy, shiny car complete with expensive rims for the wheels and top quality stereo equipment to blast music and draw further attention to ourselves. The car is then promptly driven and parked in front of an apartment. This socially accepted practice is financially backwards and lacking in long-term benefits and vision. Instead, the immediate gratification and instant visibility of being seen driving a new automobile are the first and highest priority. But perhaps, after having to grapple with a nameless, poor, and forgotten existence, this is an acceptable manner of self-reward.

In our dress we wear the clothing du jour of the most successful sports teams and name brands. No sports paraphernalia sold better in the Black community than that of Georgetown University's when they were arguably the most dominant team in college basketball in the '80s. This occurred across the country and was not just confined to Washington DC, the home of Georgetown. Sneaker companies converge on the Black community with rapid fire to have Black youth wear their newest and most innovative lines. We wear bright trinkets and gold chains, gold watches, and medallions that are larger than life as a way of getting attention and elevating our status. All are measures to establish a way to become visible and rise above the commotion.

However, the seeking of visibility, status, and value by outside enhancements instead of through an inner peace, love, and understanding of self is a problem in the Black community. Basketball, cars, designer clothing, gold trinkets, and the '90s social trend of tattoos are often attempts to mask or disguise our God-given beautiful Blackness. It is as if the Black community blames their Black skin for the problems they have experienced in life. This truly becomes a dangerous form of self-hate. The message seems to imply, 'notice me for my glitter and socially valued possessions, but please don't focus on my Blackness.'

This same dynamic and mindset is taken to play on the basketball courts. Basketball for many Black youth can become yet

55

another forum to become visible without taking an inward look at oneself. Often, self-esteem and self worth are established through the ability to win basketball games. In the Black community Black youth watch from an early age the merits, attention, and acclaim afforded Black athletes. They are basically reared on sports idolatry. The quest to reap the same value system becomes an obsession for Black youth. Consequently and unfortunately, for a majority of Black youth basketball becomes more than a game but an emotional commitment to finding one's inner self, value system, happiness, and self respect.

Thus, when Black athletes take to the courts and display acts of bravado such as hand waving and arm extensions, applauding themselves or calling for the crowd to heap praise on them after an outstanding play, it is not necessarily an intentional act of poor sportsmanship meant to embarrass or denigrate the opponent. Often it is a spontaneous outburst to say to all, "I am somebody. I can achieve and excel." Meanwhile the White power structure of the game says, "Oh, no! This can't be tolerated!" Without an understanding of the Black athlete the White power structure is uncomfortable and perhaps even fearful of this raw emotional outburst. They legislate new rules for decorum, and referees are told that this is taunting and should be penalized with a technical foul.

The emotional commitment brought to the courts by Black athletes leads to the issue of "trash talking." The distinction must be made that the White media and power structure of the game of basketball and, to a lesser degree, football coined the term "trash talking." Ironically, to label it trash talking is to imply that words between opponents have no value and are useless in the context of the play of the game. It is not true. Words are just as important as a well-placed elbow or a ferocious dunk. Words have always been an accepted practice and in fact are part of the protocol for how the game is played in the Black community. Trash talking and physical play are used to establish intimidation that, in turn, can provide an advantage in taking the victory.

Without a doubt, Muhammad Ali demonstrated the most famous and greatest example of how words could defeat an opponent. His opponents were often defeated before they entered the ring. Ali would hopelessly confuse, distract, and mentally destroy the concentration of his opponents with his verbal barrage so that his victory was usually assured before the ink was dry on the signed contract to fight.

In Black basketball verbal sparring is a real and accepted test of an opponent's will to win. It is used for two purposes. First, it is applied to gain an advantage to see if you can force an opponent to lose his concentration and confidence. Second, it is used to motivate yourself to achieve and excel, to force your will and commitment to win on your opponent. It illustrates to an opponent that you are not only the superior athlete physically, but also mentally. Words are also used to heighten your assessment of your value and self worth.

There is a line between verbal sparring and taunting. As a referee, it is my job to understand the difference. As a former Black athlete, I am less inclined to penalize trash talking. Taunting is unsportsmanlike conduct. When a player makes an outstanding play while being fouled and walks over to his opponent with an expressive and profane gesture or comment, that would be an example of taunting, and is not a part of basketball. However, telling an opponent to, "Bring it on," or "I'm going to take you to the hoop," or "You can't check me," is general verbal sparring and is a part of the game. If an opponent becomes rattled and loses focus through verbal sparring then that athlete is not mentally tough and is ripe to be taken advantage of in the pursuit of victory. It is all part of the street hustle cultivated to protect your well-being in the neighborhood. It is then brought to the court and exacted with the verbal sparring same measure as a deadly jumper or quick first step to the hoop. Verbal sparring is an ingredient brought to the city game through an attempt to establish a presence or an identity above the neighborhood environment. For Black athletes, verbal sparring is a statement of self-pride and inner confidence and a reflection of an intent to take the victory by any means necessary.

* Flair *

Black basketball is played with an unique flair. A flair that is again derived from what Black athletes bring to the game from their environment. It is a flair to be different and special; a flair to be a cut above. A flair to elevate above the invisibility of day-to-day existence. Fundamentals, while acknowledged as necessary, are nevertheless boring, faceless, and run-of-the-mill, which is akin to being invisible in society to the Black ballplayer.

Fundamentals restrict creativity and imagination, which limits individuality and personal expression. Meanwhile, flair is a distinctive declaration that gives a player an identity and independence. The flashier and more creative the move displayed by a player, the greater the flair label. Making an unconventional, anti-establishment, yet assertive and individual statement whether in sports, politics, dance or music is valued within the Black community. It is viewed as an escape from the oppression and hostile entrapment of a calculating and cold White society. Although Black youth do not understand why they seek flair they nonetheless work extremely hard to perfect it. Youth work on fancy crossovers, between the legs dribbles, and acrobatic drives to the basket to assert their individuality and independence, and not necessarily to "showoff." It is a fine line to most spectators but the reason is based on the mental issues that the Black athlete brings to the court from his environment.

Because the game is so monopolized by Black men at the professional and collegiate levels, what was once considered flashy or street ball has now melded and everyone plays pretty much the same game. However, back in the '60s and '70s you had flair if you had two ingredients. You had flair if you had a smooth, flowing game with an unflappable and calm countenance like George Gervin or Walt Frazier. They played the game effortlessly and with a reassuring cool yet they were able to control a game. The other was an explosive, abrupt, gravity defying, breathtaking game featured by a Julius "Dr. J" Erving or David Thompson.

Flair for the game in relation to Black basketball is the athlete that plays the game beyond its accepted norms. It is analogous to the street hustle: the respect given to the guy on the street that can get things done through "connections" or that can circumvent the established system to get something done. Two Black players come to mind over the last 40 years with a game or style of play that is beyond what the rules supposedly allow. Not only did they play with a style that crossed the line of what society or the game felt was allowed, but they had a Black persona. Earl "the Pearl" Monroe in the 1960's and Allen Iverson in the 2000s epitomized city flair and style.

In the '60s and '70s, Monroe had opponents and fans scratching their heads in amazement over what he could do with a basketball. The great Washington Bullets and New York Knick guard could not be defended on the basketball court. His game was novel and, many exclaimed beyond the rules. People cried that every time Earl "the Pearl" would start his yo-yo, twisting, turning and pirouetting style that he was traveling or carrying the ball. But "the Pearl" was revered in the Black community because of the anti-establishment, remarkable, flamboyant, and unconventional manner in which he played the game. His ability to play the game with a unique, innovative and personal style endeared him to the Black community. The fact that the White basketball hierarchy was confounded by his style only amplified his legend within the community. .

The same scenario is represented today by the exciting and highlight theater play of Philadelphia 76ers guard Allen Iverson. His crossover dribble and spin moves leave spellbound defenders in such a state of embarrassment and helplessness that the same clamor over travelling and carrying the ball that were present when Monroe played are again in vogue. Iverson's crossover sparked such a controversy that palming and carrying the ball by an offensive player became a point of emphasis for referees in both college and high school basketball. At referee clinics and rules interpretation meetings, the heightened concentration on carrying the ball and traveling was dubbed the "the Iverson Rule."

Interestingly, the respective backgrounds of these two men also have a lot to do with why they are embraced and viewed as icons by the Black community. The backgrounds of the two men helped to bond them exclusively to the Black community without fear of a "crossover" appeal that would force us to share their legend with White folks. They are often considered too "Black." The same type of aura that made James Brown's music solely appreciated by the Black community and not adopted by mainstream America until the late '80s.

Monroe had the nickname of "Black Jesus." He was born and raised in the ghetto of Philadelphia. He attended a Black college, Winston Salem State, and played for legendary Black coach Clarence "Big House" Gaines. His legend and game grew from his summers played in the famed Rucker League in New York City. Earl was a very dark skinned man with a tall Afro haircut. When first drafted by the Baltimore Bullets, it seemed like the perfect fit between player and city. Baltimore, a blue collar town in love with basketball and in search of an icon, meshed uniquely with "the Pearl's" persona and style of play.

Iverson, meanwhile was raised poor in Newport News, Virginia. He had an infamous racial incident with the law and, had it not been for the interjection of then Virginia governor L. Douglas Wilder, he quite possibly would never have had a collegiate or professional career. When you discuss Iverson's incident with Black people they will almost unanimously tell you that his charges were bogus and extreme, yet typical for a Black person involved in a racial incident south of the Mason-Dixon line.

When Iverson attended Georgetown, his legend and status as a symbol of Black pride became stamped with authenticity. He was at Georgetown where, theory says, only the hardcore players of the game attended. Georgetown, coached by the controversial and powerful John Thompson, had long been adopted by the Black community as its university. When Iverson attended Georgetown two absolutes were known: Iverson would not have any off the court troubles and his glittering game would shine even brighter and grow even larger under Coach Thompson's watch and tutelage. Iverson left college after two years to become the number one pick in the NBA draft. Now, the multi-tattooed, braided hair, unconventional dressing Iverson totally intimidates and offends a segment of White America which fails to acknowledge his MVP-winning, first-team-all-star talent. They are so preoccupied with his outward appearance that they totally fail to grasp one of the toughest, most intense, and dominant players the NBA has ever known.

* Intimidation *

Physical play, emotion, and flair are distinctive characteristics that shape Black basketball. They are methods for the Black athlete to express his individuality. However, intimidation is how the game of basketball is won. To define intimidation in the game of Black basketball first there is an understanding by the participants that victory is not won, but taken. Winning the game is determined by the highest score after time has expired. Taking the victory is jagged and confrontational. It is a way of thinking that says the victory will come with any price or measure necessary to win. Intimidation is foremost in determining who wins and who loses in the game of Black basketball.

Most of the athletes on the playgrounds have huge talents. They have all the shots, the creative moves off the dribble, the high rising jumping ability and more, so winning becomes a distinction of who wants it the most. This, in turn, brings in the intangibles of the heart and head and this is where intimidation steps to the forefront. There are all types of intimidation. In fact, in the big city intimidation is understood and is considered as much a part of the game as a silky smooth jump shot or crossover dribble. In the Black community the competition level is very keen so another criteria has to be sought out to give your team leverage. The team with the biggest heart and will to compete will ultimately win the game. The team that best handles the inevitable elements of intimidation will take the victory. In no team sport is the will to win and to conquer intimidation more apparent than in basketball.

There are several reasons why intimidation is so visible in basketball including the close proximity between the players and the spectators. It is the way the players are dressed in glorified underwear, physically and emotionally exposed for all to judge. It is also the fast pace and intensity of the game that is highlighted and featured by the one-on-one, man-to-man contests of wills that occur almost every trip up and down the court.

Great players thrive on attempts by others to intimidate them and they elevate their games to an even higher level of efficiency. Indeed, they turn the tables and exact an even higher measure of intimidation on their opponents. Good players ignore intimidation and let their games speak. Average players let intimidation strip them of their concentration and they seek retaliation. When confronted with intimidation potentially competent but faint of heart players mentally and physically freeze, become scared and tentative, and are almost useless in the pursuit of victory. Thus, every game becomes a seek and destroy mission to find a weak minded opponent. Simply stated, intimidation is about manhood and sending a message, gaining an advantage and establishing turf or a superior presence.

How Basketball Is Played in the Black Community

Most spectators and avid fans of basketball underestimate the importance of intimidation. Perhaps their only reference point for understanding intimidation is when announcers and commentators speak of playing a game on the road in a hostile environment and how a crowd can unnerve an opponent. By in large, a hostile crowd doesn't intimidate opposing players as much as it provides energy to the home team. Rowdy crowds do not intimidate Black players. Their day-to-day surroundings are far tougher than any gymnasium. Clearly, it is the man-on-man intimidation within the game that really determines who will take the victory.

It took becoming a referee and going in and out of gyms to officiate basketball on all levels—high school, AAU, recreation, men's leagues, summer leagues, and college—for me to see the importance that intimidation plays within the game. Not every player can play to intimidate. Not every player understands that victory is taken. I have come to understand that you must have a deep passion for the game of basketball, an unrestrained fire and a contempt for losing to want to exact intimidation on your opponent to win. This has often been interpreted as a "hard edge" or "mean streak," but it is clearly a trait played out on the court primarily by ball players who are raised in tough, unforgiving surroundings. These are athletes that do not make a distinction between an opponent and an enemy. This trait is associated with Black athletes that have lived with pain and have had to do without things in life, such as food and shelter, safety and a family support system. They fight to be heard, shed invisibility, and establish their own individuality.

When the Black athlete takes to the court and realizes that he has the skills to play the game of basketball at a high and proficient level he wants the success, accolades, and victory that he has not found on a consistent level in his life. To ensure the peace and rewarding success of victory, especially when contrasted with losing, which reminds him of his day-to-day struggle, he will use any measure at his disposal to continue winning. Obtaining the victory in a ballgame becomes a badge, a medal of honor to Black youth whose victories in life are infrequent, hazy, short-lived and of minimal long-term value. The act of intimidation in big city basketball is an attempt to illustrate to an opponent that your will and desire to win is greater than his. It is an attempt to make your opponent mentally fearful of, and inferior to, your capabilities and talents. Intimidation is exercised physically, athletically, visually, and verbally.

* Physical Intimidation *

I have witnessed physical, athletic, and verbal intimidation. Physical intimidation is synonymous with Black basketball, but it is also the area of basketball that most concerns the power structure of the game. However, contrary to what the establishment and hierarchy believe, physical intimidation does not lead to fights. Players want to play the game. It is not their intent to be banished from the game. Physical intimidation is plainly about testing an opponent's heart or manhood. It is about seeing if an opponent has the will to take the victory and not just about the skill level to play the game.

As a referee, I have witnessed that physical intimidation usually manifests itself early in the first and third quarters of games. That is when elbows fly, hard picks are set or hard fouls occur as a player drives to the basket. These are plays of physical contact to try to send a message to the opponent that tonight's game will be intense and, if necessary, will be about survival of the fittest. A lot of times coaches do not mind a hard foul and do not care if an intentional or technical foul is called. They believe that early in the game a foul can be overcome and the message sent in terms of intimidation is well worth the penalty. The foul becomes an attempt to establish the tougher team. As the referee, I have no problem with this strategy and I penalize the transgressor accordingly. However, in the second and fourth quarters of games, intimidation usually takes a back seat to execution, trying to exploit the weaknesses of your opponent and winning the game. The game shifts to a different dynamic where the goal is clearly to win the game.

I had a conversation with an excellent coach, Richard Jackson, formerly of Phelps Vocational High School in northeast Washington DC. He told me that as part of his game plan, especially when his teams would play outside of the Washington metropolitan area where the perception of his all Black team was that they were overaggressive, he would call a special play known as "Kentucky." The play would call for all five players to play tight man-to-man defense and, on his signal from the bench, foul the opponent at the same time. His rationale was that since the other team had made a natural predetermination that his team was aggressive he would attempt to turn that thought into intimidation to rattle the other team and gain an advantage. The referee could only call one foul, yet every opposing player would be hit and the message would be delivered for the rest of the game.

At its most elementary level, physical intimidation is going to the courts and testing the heart of your opponent to see if he is physically able to do whatever it takes to win a ball game. The will to win in some players and the intimidation to strip other players can sometimes be detected as early as the jump ball at the start of the game. I have looked in the eyes of some teams before the game and could easily and correctly predict which team wants to take the victory. Most people want to associate physical play with football because each play results in contact. It is why the players are well padded with helmets and suits of armor. However, basketball is also all about physical contact. The speed, pace, and intensity of the game, combined with the immense pride that the big city player takes with him to the court, and his willingness to take the victory ensures physical contact will occur. In addition, the playgrounds have taught the player that physical contact is an acceptable part of the game. Toss into the mix the Black athlete's frustrations and confrontational environment and a physical game is considered a normal and preferred way of playing the game.

Similar to physical intimidation is verbal intimidation. This is when players talk repeatedly in an attempt to mentally distract, unnerve, and weaken their opponents. If verbal sparring can lead to a player becoming unnerved, agitated, afraid, and incapable of playing to the best of his abilities, it will be used to take the victory.

The mostly White announcers, legislators and rules interpreters of the game of basketball want the game to be played on a plane devoid of all types of intimidation. However, Black youth, the main participants of the game of basketball, do not live their life away from the court on a level playing field and it is presumptuous to think that the big city athlete would play the game in a manner different from his day-to-day existence. One lesson the Black ballplayer has been taught better than most through life experiences off the court is that life in this society is not played on a level playing field. Black athletes bring to the game an attitude of taking what they want, of taking the victory by any way possible.

* Athletic Intimidation *

A dominant player on the court portrays athletic intimidation. This is a player whose will and fearlessness of heart parallels his already superior athletic skill. This particular player has physical gifts and attributes so exceptional to other players that his sheer presence can break the opponent's spirit. This unique player can carry his team to victory through his physical skills. Just as important, he can lift his team to victory through his competitive spirit and will to win. It is a presence or athletic arrogance that provides a protective foundation of confidence to his teammates and invokes an insecure anxiety in his opponents. It is a rare player that can exhibit such athletic intimidation that you know as a spectator, opposing player, coach, and referee that something that he has done or will do will set the tone for the rest of the game. It is a combination of athletic prowess, competitive zeal, and an attitude of fearlessness mixed with a mercenary heart that can intimidate an opponent and ensure victory.

Perhaps the single best illustration of athletic intimidation occurred in what many call the most important game in American sports, the1966 NCAA championship game between Texas Western University, starting five Black players against an all-White team from the University of Kentucky. An early thunderous dunk by Texas Western's forward David "Big Daddy" Lattin was considered pivotal in sending a message that Texas Western would not be denied. Observers at the game including Miami Heat coach, Pat Riley, and Tommy Kron, teammates on that Kentucky team, admit that Kentucky appeared to be intimidated. Texas Western won 72-65 in a game that permanently changed collegiate sports, especially basketball. The intimidating impact of "Big Daddy" Lattin's dunks went far beyond the '66 championship game. Frank Fitzpatrick in his book, *And the Walls Came Tumbling Down*, writes, "Less than a year after Lattin's dunks so forcefully punctuated Texas Western's championship, the NCAA Rules Committee banned the shot. The all-White committee at first portrayed the move as an attempt to prevent injuries and equipment damage, citing 1,500 cases in the previous few seasons. Then they called it an effort to preserve basketball's integrity." However, Fitzpatrick says, "the ban was nothing more than an attempt to stifle the dominating presence of big, strong, threatening, Black stars such as Lattin and Lew Alcindor as other rules had earlier attempted to stop Wilt Chamberlain and Bill Russell. The dunk was absent from college basketball for 10 years."

In athletic intimidation, the key ingredient is having the combination of athletic talent and mental toughness. An absence of one or the other simply makes one a good player but incapable of athletic intimidation. This is especially true for Black youth that play the game on the scholastic and college levels. There is not much they haven't seen on the basketball court. There are more talented players on the playgrounds that have never played high school or college basketball. The playgrounds are filled with legends that can and have done marvelous things on a basketball court. So, it is not solely athletic gifts that lead to athletic intimidation. Nor is it physical size or physical stature, being the tallest or strongest or quickest or highest jumping, that can provide athletic intimidation. Again, the streets of the Black community are filled with players that can jump and pluck the proverbial quarter off the top of a backboard or dunk with such velocity that the rim separates from the backboard, or guys that are so quick they leave would-be defenders grasping for air then come back and get them for the ride to the rim.

Athletic intimidation is also about timing. It occurs in a game when tensions are high and nerves are raw. Often it is when lesser players wilt and search for another player to seize the moment. This moment does not have to be the last shot in the last quarter. It can happen at any point in the course of a game. The moment could come after a heated exchange between players. Or it could occur after a team has taken the momentum of the game and forged a lead or made a dramatic comeback. It can even occur early in the first quarter when a player's performance is so outstanding that everyone can tell that this special player will not let his team be denied tonight. In essence, athletic intimidation is exacted by an exceptional athlete with toughness and heart performing a superior athletic feat at the appropriate and crucial time in a game, which usually makes the difference between winning and losing.

* Athletic Arrogance *

For an athlete to be capable of athletic intimidation he must combine physical skills with an undeniable competitive spirit and will to succeed. He must have an athletic arrogance, an inner knowledge that his physical and athletic skills extend beyond any opponent and obstacle he will encounter in athletic competition. Athletic arrogance goes beyond just a belief in your athletic skills. It is a mind-set of egotism and conceitedness in which an athlete knows he will be successful against any and all odds. Most athletes think they are good. In fact most have an exaggerated opinion of their talents. But for most athletes, this is false bravado and, indeed, when the lights shine brightest and winning is on the line, they often fail the challenge.

Another small group of athletes knows they are athletically superior and have answered the call and took the victory. However, they lack focus, discipline, and commitment off the court to achieve their full athletic potential. This is often why the playgrounds of the big city are filled with athletic legends. Meanwhile, an even smaller percentage of athletes understand their tremendous gifts, know with a single-mindedness that they are superior, and have the athletic arrogance and competitive ego to force their will and talent to take the victory and intimidate an opponent.

This is why I marvel at the Black athletes that excel in sports, especially those that play basketball. While White America flippantly dismisses the Black athlete's success as natural or God-given, I understand the hardships they have endured to reach their potential. Athletic arrogance is mental toughness, intelligence, and discipline borne of hard work, dedication, determination, and success. For Black athletes to claim athletic arrogance amid all the turmoil, poverty, racism, invisibility, and low self-esteem inherent in growing up in the Black community, is a tremendous accomplishment and should never be taken lightly, especially by our own people.

When I referee games that put me in a position to witness these talented and mentally focused athletes compete and exact their style of intimidation during the course of a game, it is a beautiful thing to watch.

I had the fortunate experience to referee a basketball game featuring Kobe Bryant, then a high school senior. Bryant was playing in a showcase AAU and NCAA sanctioned fall tournament called the Charlie Webber Invitational Tournament held each September on the campus of the University of Maryland. Over 60 AAU and high school teams from all across the country came to compete in the three-day tournament.

The Charlie Webber Tournament, like the NIKE camp or ABCD camp, is an easy venue for college coaches to see the top prospects in one confined area, matching their skills against the best competition from other areas of the country. It is held in September so the college coaches can evaluate athletes one more time before the signing period for athletes to pick a college in November.

At the time, I did not know Bryant was one of the players in the game. Nor did I know he was the consensus number one player in the nation for the upcoming season. However, it did not take long for this tremendous athlete to stand above the others with his basketball skills. Bryant proceeded to put on a dazzling display of all-around basketball. Despite being the tallest player on his team at 6'5," Bryant played all five positions on the floor. He jumped center at the opening tap. He rebounded, and hit NBA distance three point shots. He beat the other team's full court press with his passing and ball handling skills. He made his free throws and open jump shots while alternately driving to the basket to find open teammates. Most important and impressive to me was how he scrapped and competed. With his basketball future brightest among the bright, Bryant could have coasted. Instead he dived for loose balls going out of bounds or plunged into a fray of players on the floor for a loose ball. He played defense pridefully and passionately. Bryant scored 36 points in the game.

As I worked the game, his athletic arrogance was omnipresent. He was able to athletically intimidate the opponent and he played with a passion and an assassin's heart that was a pleasure to behold. He verbally challenged the opponent, his teammates, and even had a word or two for the referees, however respectful. I recall when I played ball that I never competed with an egotistical spirit and perhaps it is why I appreciated watching him perform. Clearly, Bryant was the premier player on the floor. Watching the game unfold, I knew there would be a point in the game when Bryant would exact athletic intimidation that probably would stamp the game as his and take the victory.

In the fourth quarter of this close game, Bryant drove baseline from right to left. As he dribbled underneath the basket with his right hand he gathered himself and the ball. He leaped out diagonally from underneath the basket in front of the backboard while twisting his body to use his back as a shield to keep the defender from the ball. While still in the air he raised the ball from his waist to about shoulder height in shooting formation. As a second defender came over to contest the shot, Bryant, while still in the air, double clutched the ball, took a hit from the confused defender, released the ball with an extension of his arms and wrist and gently laid the ball against the backboard and into the basket. All the while drawing the foul from the defender.

As my referee partner called the foul and proceeded to the scorers table to report the violation, it was my responsibility to line the players up for the upcoming free throw. Bryant, knowing that the play was during a crucial point in the game and he had bested a less talented but bigger opponent, pounced on the moment to intimidate. As players gathered around the play, Bryant, heading for the free throw line, brushed against a couple of opposing players in his path with raised elbows. The move was not malicious or forceful enough to merit a technical foul, but it was indeed purposeful. It was a message and an attempt to intimidate beyond athletic play. Most of the players noticed. As the referee, I understood my need to tell Bryant sternly that I would not tolerate overzealous displays. However, as a fan of basketball I also understood what exactly had transpired and why I secretly derived great joy from the encounter.

CHAPTER FIVE:
Georgetown Basketball: A Local and National Phenomenon

There is no way possible to have a discussion about basketball and its impact on Black youth, especially with Washington DC as the backdrop, without including Georgetown University basketball and Hall of Fame coach, John Thompson. Throughout the decades of the '70s and '80s, no greater allegiance was formed in sports than between Georgetown basketball and the Black community. Georgetown basketball was the epitome of what Black basketball was all about. John Thompson, in my opinion, is probably the greatest Black sports figure in terms of his positive influence and example to the Black community since Muhammad Ali. What Muhammad Ali did for Black folks in the '60s and '70s in this nation in terms of giving us pride, visibility, and excellence in performance, John Thompson equaled with Georgetown basketball for 27 years from 1972 until his retirement in 1999.

John Thompson, large in stature standing 6'10" and over 300 pounds, forceful, loud, confrontational, and Black, created his Georgetown teams to duplicate his persona. The Georgetown teams were big, strong, intimidating, and aggressive. They broke the mold of how college basketball was played in the '70s and '80s. Thompson and his teams gave fuel to Black youths that their style of playing basketball was indeed a winning style. Generations of Black youth grew up wanting to play for Georgetown. From Washington DC and cities on the East coast to Los Angeles, California and all municipalities in between, youth wore Georgetown paraphernalia. Georgetown gear and apparel was the number one choice bought by Black youth from coast to coast, including professional sports teams. Generations of Black youth grew up playing and rejoicing in the style of ball played by Georgetown. The Georgetown style was a comfort zone that was identical to the way Black athletes played the game on the playgrounds of the Black community. Thanks to the success of Georgetown the Black style, often criticized for being confrontational, out of control, and overly aggressive, now had to be labeled as winning.

Georgetown showed the nation that its style of basketball, which resembled the way of living for Black youth, was indeed a successful way to play basketball. Many are quick to attribute Georgetown's popularity to the fact that its teams were predominately Black youth from the big city headed by a Black coach. Yet others dismissed their popularity as bandwagon folk that naturally ride the wave of a winner. Another explanation centered on the fact that Georgetown seemed to be on television nightly due to the timely marriage of cable and the Big East conference corresponding with the heightened popularity of college basketball and its March Madness marketing. Indeed, all were factors for Georgetown's rising popularity in the Black community.

However, the groundswell of pride within the big city associated with Georgetown basketball is far deeper than the racial composition of its players and coaches, its exposure on television or even its winning tradition. It was the style and manner in which Georgetown won that placed the Hoyas on a pedestal.

Georgetown basketball was validation to the Black athlete, both young and old, that the Black way of playing basketball was now a winning way of playing basketball. Black basketball was no longer "ghetto ball" or undisciplined or fundamentally unsound or any of the other adjectives that described city ball as a helter-skelter, unrestrained, showoff style of play with its only true place of value on the playgrounds of the big cities. Georgetown shattered that myth. And with great pride Georgetown basketball reached icon status in the Black communities.

When John Thompson started at Georgetown in 1972, the top team in local college basketball was the University of Maryland, coached by Lefty Driesell. Maryland was successful and popular, had tradition and played in the pristine and esteemed Atlantic Coast

Conference. Maryland had outstanding players such as John Lucas, Tom McMillian, Len Elmore, Moe Howard, and Brad Davis. But gradually, Georgetown eroded their fan base. As Georgetown began to win there was a transformation in Washington. Ironically, Maryland through the years had just as many Black athletes as Georgetown. In fact, Maryland had several athletes from its backyard of Washington DC and Baltimore. Lefty Driesell was an excellent recruiter and usually got the city ballplayers he coveted. Yet Georgetown, because of its heartfelt and intense style was still the emerging force and had the yeoman's share of public sentiment and support within the Black neighborhoods of Washington DC. While racial composition was a constant and huge consideration for Georgetown's popularity, the style of basketball played by the Hoyas should not be minimized. Georgetown's popularity should not be defined exclusively in Black and White terms.

There were other successful college programs that featured Black athletes and various styles of play, but none could wrestle away the hold of Georgetown as the team of choice of big city youth. The University of Louisville with the fabulous moniker "Doctors of Dunk" won championships with predominately Black players displaying high-flying, entertaining, big city flair. The University of Houston with the greatest basketball nickname ever, "Phi Slamma Jamma," dunked its way with athletic Black players such as Clyde "the Glide" Drexler to several Final Fours but never captivated the pulse of the big city in comparison to Georgetown. The University of Nevada Las Vegas in the '90s and Marquette University in the late '70s were coached by street-wise toughs Jerry Tarkanian and Al McGuire, had predominately rough and tumble Black athletes on their teams and won national championships, but never matched Georgetown's devoted following.

University of Arkansas won a title in the '90s with a Black coach, Nolan Richardson, playing full court brand of ball dubbed by its coach as "40 minutes of hell." But perhaps since Arkansas' success

75

came after Georgetown and because it was a deep south, rural school, a constant reminder of painful days of yesterday for Black folk, it was never embraced as a big city team.

In the 27 years that Georgetown was led by John Thompson only one university in college basketball could challenge the Hoyas popularity. In the early '90s, The University of Michigan featuring the hip and trendy "Fab Five," overtook Georgetown in merchandise and apparel sales to Black youth. The team, led by Chris Webber, Jalen Rose, Juwan Howard, Ray Jackson, and Jim King played a pulsating, freewheeling, no fear, cool under pressure brand of ball that was mesmerizing. The "Fab Five" were freshman and sophomores with an attitude, but had enough talent to cash any check their countenance and mouth could write. They spoke their mind, yet were articulate and poised in how they communicated. The group would go to back-to-back Final Fours.

The timing of their climb to overtake Georgetown was perfect. They had an egoless, good coach in Steve Fisher who did not attempt to stifle or repress the spirit and instincts of his youthful assemblage. Georgetown was struggling for its personality—caught between the Alonzo Mourning era, which had just ended, and before anyone knew there would be an Allen Iverson era. The only consideration that would support Georgetown remaining as King of the Black sports culture was the fact that Michigan's "Fab Five" duration was brief and they failed to win a championship. Webber, Howard and Rose left school for early entry to the NBA and the "Fab Five" era descended just as rapidly as it climbed, probably never to be duplicated again in college basketball.

High school and youth league coaches, instead of tweaking or silently altering the Black style game as was previously done in the alleged name of success, found it okay to play the Georgetown style of play—full court, aggressive and attacking, waves of fresh players off the bench, committed to taking the victory. The brand of ball exhibited by Georgetown was now boldly trumpeted as successful.

Georgetown Basketball: A Local and National Phenomenon

The single dramatic change in the game of basketball that I have noticed over the last four decades is the faster speed of the game. It is not necessarily the speed of the players which has increased, but the style, pace, and tempo of the game itself. It is a more aggressive, up-tempo brand of ball, offensively and defensively. I am referring specifically to boys club, youth league, high school and college. Georgetown University basketball was the pioneer for this transformation.

The Georgetown way and its success completely changed how the game was viewed by fans, taught by coaches, and executed by players. Youth would come to the games wearing Georgetown apparel. A new breed of young innovative coaches from boys clubs to AAU to high school implemented Georgetown's aggressive full court pressure and multiple substitutions. It is amazing to referee a game and watch the volumes of boys club, youth league, AAU and high school teams and programs that still call out "Georgetown" as a defensive scheme or play during the course of a ballgame. In a word, the Georgetown style of play was aggressive. Georgetown would not let any team dictate pace, tempo, physical play, etc. Georgetown basketball was about taking the victory. This is why Georgetown basketball galvanized the Black community.

John Thompson was a product of the tough streets of Washington DC. As a high school player, he won city championships with Archbishop Carroll High. After a successful college career at Providence, including an NIT championship, he won two championships with the Boston Celtics. As a coach at St. Anthony's high school in Washington D.C. Thompson compiled a record of 122-28. Thompson was a winner at every level of the game.

One thing John Thompson knew was that basketball was more than high-flying dunks and fancy crossover dribbles. He knew that it was about an attitude, a mindset, about heart. He knew that basketball was about pride and a test of manhood. He knew the game was about intimidation. John Thompson never bought into the concept that Black athletes were undisciplined showboat artists. He went beyond the athletic skill to see the inner man, and with his background as a player and educator he knew what it took to mold big city athletes into a cohesive winning unit.

Many say that Georgetown came into prominence only after the recruitment of Patrick Ewing. Yet Thompson was a winner at St. Anthony's high school employing the same style that he would utilize later at Georgetown. His teams at St. Anthony's were aggressive with a "take the victory" attitude. Six players from Thompson's last championship team at St. Anthony's would eventually follow him to Georgetown. Georgetown's no fear, aggressive attitude of taking the victory was wholly endorsed in the big city. As the teams won, Georgetown's program gathered respect and exposure. Soon the Hoyas were able to sign the best ballplayers from around the county. With the advent of the Big East conference and the increasing popularity of college basketball as a televised sport, Georgetown became a regular on cable television. The Georgetown way became a national phenomenon.

In taking the victory Georgetown teams would use any strategy and weaponry at its disposal to win. Georgetown would lay claim to the hard work, no frills, and intangibles of the game. Rebounding, defense, and controlling loose balls were the first priorities in winning basketball. Every game would become an endurance test of willpower and mental toughness. The Hoyas, with their physical play and endless stream of substitutions of fresh players, attempted to make each game a battle of attrition. Shooting the basketball and making free throws often seemed to be an afterthought for the Hoyas players. It often appeared that scoring points came from any player that could force a turnover or gather a rebound from the opposition.

Georgetown games, because of their endless stream of substitutions and their aggressive end-to-end, physical play resulting in unlimited free throws and fouls, were often marathon sessions in unlimited free throws and fouls, were often marathon sessions with both fans and players alike exhausted by game's end. If tempers were to flare due to the heightened emotions and physical confrontation, this was fine with Georgetown. When there was an altercation with one Georgetown player, it was an altercation with all of Georgetown's players. The players from the Hoya bench would spring instantly from the sidelines to aid their comrade in a fracas. The players were totally unified and committed to each other. While fighting was never condoned, even opposing rival coaches such as the legendary Lou Carnasecca at St. Johns University admitted to the press that he secretly admired how the Georgetown team would stand united and protect each other against any opposition or obstacle. The coach knew that this close knit kinship was a factor in why Georgetown won.

Interestingly enough, due to Georgetown's intimidating and physical style and propensity for fighting many of the rules in place within college and high school basketball were changed. Rules on bench decorum, players leaving the bench area to participate in a fight, game suspensions for fighting, technical fouls and intentional fouls for unsportsmanlike conduct were rewritten or added in part because of the Hoya way of basketball. As a referee, I feel the rules were mostly correct and necessary for the betterment of the game. As a basketball fan, I admired Georgetown's unity and no fear, resilient spirit. Yet, for all the good messages Georgetown basketball sent to athletes, non-violence was not one of them. There were too many instances when intense games decayed into ugly melees and the sight of bloodied jerseys and bandaged athletes was not a positive projection.

Georgetown basketball was not about outscoring its opponent. The Hoya focus was on wearing down and stripping an opponent's will to compete, and it featured a large dose of intimidation. In the late '70s and early '80s, Georgetown's typical game would entail a fairly close contest with about 10 minutes remaining in the second half. Then the Hoyas with their aggressive attitude and will-to-win would hit another gear and pull away from an opposition that seemed to be deflated and lose its desire to compete. Georgetown would ultimately win games by 10, 12, 15 points or better.

The timing could have not been more perfect. In the '60s, the Black community watched and became proud of how we, could compete and be successful in sports against the White athlete, especially in basketball. Then, Georgetown came along in the '70s and took our awareness and our style to yet an even higher level of understanding and self-respect. Georgetown told a nation that Black athletes need not repress the aggressiveness learned on the streets, dispelled the myth that Black folk could not unify for a common cause, and most of all demonstrated that a Black man could captain the ship to victory in battle.

Moreover, Georgetown's greatest accomplishment did not take place on the basketball court. John Thompson's athletes at Georgetown graduated from the university. Ninety-seven percent of the athletes that played four years at Georgetown during Thompson's 27 years as coach earned their degrees. This was a tremendous feat in a climate of college basketball where Black athletes in particular were used solely for their athletic gifts, neglected academically, and cast adrift with an insincere thank you but without a degree when their eligibility expired. Georgetown's graduation rate was a huge positive message conveyed to big city youth that if you want it you could achieve it despite your current situation in life. This was a huge source of pride and inspiration to Black communities across our nation.

CHAPTER SIX:
Attraction to Addiction: Finding the Proper Balance with Basketball

In the Black community, no other endeavor generates attention and acclaim as quickly as athletic success. Black youth see the rewards and accolades that are tied to athletic success. The launching pad to success in the Black community has often been through athletic accomplishment. Black boys are all too ready to accept and chase the mantle of athletic stardom. Soon the chase consumes them and what starts as an attraction becomes an all-out addiction to athletic gratification. For Black youth, the primary sport of choice is basketball.

Unfortunately, even at the youth level it appears that basketball has taken on a big business aura and an accelerated pace for athletes to achieve recognition. This in turn places a hefty amount of unnecessary pressure on young athletes to perform at too early an age. Balance and perspective is compromised promoting an all-or-nothing relationship with the sport. It is an unsettling change that I have watched in youth sports, contrary to growing up in the '60s where athletic success started on a smaller scale.

For example, prior to the sneaker wars, "March Madness," cable television and multi-million dollar contracts, sports participation was a natural and straightforward progression. You would play in your neighborhood. Then you would play against and with the older boys, the teenagers, and if you could compete on their level the word would get around that you could play the game and that you were somebody on the fast track to sports success. Then you would play opposing neighborhoods and word would continue to spread. Once in school you would continue to play informally at first, on the playgrounds in the morning before class or during lunch or in PE class. Again, word of your success or athletic skill would begin to buzz around the community. With each successful venture came an increased sense of confidence, self-worth, and self-esteem. Each time you were chosen first in pick up games or hit the game- winning shot or were told that you were special, another log would go onto the fire and passion to succeed in sports.

In the Black community, athletic accomplishment is the number one way of standing above the fray and receiving acclaim. As a seventh grader attending St. Francis Xavier Catholic School in southeast DC, I remember the influence of sports. Walking home after school the neighborhood boys, who perceived us as privileged, spoiled kids whose parents had money, would occasionally hang on the corner and threaten us if we did not give them any money. On one particular day I unknowingly walked straight into the path of a group of five or six local toughs seeking funds. A member of the group that I had played basketball with told the others that I was cool and to back off. I was exempt from extortion and intimidation because of my athletic prowess. Having that type of popularity, notoriety, and standing made it very easy for me and my Black male peers to continue our focus on sports.

Eventually, this type of sports legacy followed athletes to junior high, high school and then hopefully college and beyond. Sports participation was less defined or structured but athletes still ascended through sports to a level above the fray. The dream remained the same but the pace of the sports train was more conducive to maintaining a better balance between sports and life off the court or field. The major difference was the absence of the glare and intensity of the spotlight that today's youth must deal with at such a young age.

Today, there are cable television shows devoted solely to high school athletics. You have the *USA Today* newspaper which ranks the top 25 teams in several sports and provides us with a region to region geographical recap of sporting activity. Prior to 1982, there wasn't a *USA Today*. Now, many national sports magazines rate the top scholastic players starting with athletes in the seventh grade. As has always been the case there are local high school rankings in the local city newspapers, but today the sports section has several pages of complete coverage. There are local television programs that have 30-minute shows devoted to local high school sports, complete with games and athletes of the week. ESPN and ESPN2 televise several national high school all-star games in prime time, complete with announcers gushing about the tremendous untapped potential of seventeen and eighteen year olds.

There are tout sheets and Internet sports services that rank, rate and predict the college choices of the athletes. They chart the points and performances of the athletes not only during the season, but also during the summer basketball camps and all-star games and AAU tournaments. There is an overabundance of summer basketball instruction camps and invitation only camps, summer basketball leagues and even fall leagues that keep athletes playing structured basketball without a break.

In the '70s, there was no such creation as a fall basketball league for high school players. Young athletes in the big city are now playing basketball games year round. Many will play upwards of 60 to 80 basketball games in the spring and summer months between the normal school basketball seasons from November through February. The scope of athletic participation is totally out of control and the disparity between sport and a balanced life for young adults is as wide as a canyon and growing wider each season.

Is the end in sight? Hardly. Fox Television is laying the foundation for a nationally televised high school football playoff and championship. Under this avalanche of opportunities to compete, youth follow the lead of parents and adults and pursue athletic stardom and success passionately and completely. For Black youth sports, and basketball in particular, become the only way, instead of an additional way, to have a successful and productive future.

On the surface many will say that exposure and structured league activity are good for Black athletes without adequate alternatives. That opinion can only come from a childless adult or one that is making a profit from the games the athletes play. The proliferation of youth and scholastic sports continues and children are starting out younger and younger, first and foremost because it is profitable. From the national cable television to the local newspaper, high school sports coverage has increased becaues of money, not for the humanitarian ideal of focusing on children. It is a trickle down theory that started with the country's thirst for athletic competition. ESPN and its stations as well as other sports oriented cable stations have open slots for programming. With professional sports and college sports coverage saturated, the next choice is to filter down to high school sports. This easily explains one of the reasons why the McDonalds All-American boy's basketball game is shown in prime time by ESPN.

Already, cable networks and their print cousin *USA Today*, cover sports on a national level and scope that the local media can't compete with. As the local news stations lose sports viewers to the expansive coverage provided by the sports cable channels their only niche and advantage becomes a greater focus on local sports, particularly high school sports. Again it's a profit driven concept. From a business standpoint, it is understand-able and acceptable, but it should not be interpreted as a community effort to save our youth.

Futhermore, many of the founders of the multitude of summer basketball camps and leagues and tournaments should not receive Hall of Fame status as beacons of the community. Often they only provide a cheap, ill-conceived, unsafe and unaccountable product for the athletes. Yet, their recurring theme is: "We are keeping youth off the streets." What many are really doing is making a quick hit-and-run buck off the hard working, cash strapped, time-consumed, caring parent who is fearful of the abundance of summer free time for their children. The increased volume of basketball camps, leagues and tournaments is no different than the copycat tendencies of a good idea that hits any other business. In one spring morning edition of the *Washington Post* sports page there were nine advertisements for youth participation in basketball summer camps, summer leagues, and AAU or other sponsored tournaments. Don't be fooled. So many advertisements in one day for youth basketball participation, three weeks before school is out is primarily about adults getting paid. So, buyer beware! It is not always about the young athlete. Many of these coordinators and self-appointed directors of summer camps and leagues know that parents either buy into the athletic success and potential of their children or are concerned about the dangers of the street. Either way they know that parents will do whatever they must to get their athlete enrolled, short of a background check on the camp or league director.

Today, most high schools participate in a summer basketball league. They are usually handled through the school coach. If you feel comfortable with the coach then trust his judgment. But do not forfeit summer vacations and family outings just so the youth can play summer basketball. Keep the right perspective of family first. Sadly, even the other scholastic sports are jumping on the more-is-better bandwagon and starting their athletic seasons in the summer. High schools are starting many of their sports programs such as football and soccer seasons earlier each year. Thus, practices are starting as much as to three weeks before school starts in late summer, ultimately forcing families to alter or even cancel summer vacations. Clearly, not only has sports usurped academics, but it is now commandeering family bonding, values, and time.

Sometimes the biggest problem for young athletes, is the unrealistic aspirations of parents and guardians. Black parents are four times more likely than Whites to believe their athlete is headed for a professional career. The parents' dreams for the athlete is often more unrealistic than those of the players. This is another undue stress on the young athlete and another unnecessary, push toward a feast or famine relationship with a given sport. All three circumstances—the overexposure from the media, the abundance of opportunities to compete, and the pressure to live up to the expectations of others—force Black athletes toward an addictive relationship with basketball.

Clearly, bigger does not necessarily mean better. There are more sports organizations and more exposure and opportunities, but it is evident that the end product is not always a better all-around athlete and person. Player development and fundamentals are a distant memory. True, Black youth are participating in bigger and more structured organizations, but winning is the priority over player development. Meanwhile the youngsters take to the courts with a methodical, matter-of-fact attitude of what the game can do for them rather than an actual passion for the game. Perhaps because of the surplus of games and adults clamoring for their services, youth in the Black community play the game with an expressionless formality usually reserved for men and women working a daily 9 to 5 job. This is especially true for the endless spring and summer leagues and tournaments. I wonder if the athletes are plain and simple having fun. It is very noticeable that their skills are not improving, but I wonder if the athletes still honestly enjoy the game. It seems that fun and enjoyment have become a casualty as young athlete's big time motivations and adults' personal agendas move to the forefront and drown out the pure pleasure of sport.

As athletes compete almost year round what happens to individual work and improvement of their games? This is especially applicable in the summers when athletes have the best opportunity to improve on their weaknesses. Instead athletes are traveling from city to city, tournament to tournament, game to game in pursuit of the best competition, exposure, and recognition. Practice is held merely to meet your new teammates and install a couple of fundamental plays.

In fact, players' priorities have made almost a 180° turn from 20 years ago. It sometimes appears that athletes now play in the winter just to stay in shape for the summer seasons. When I played high school basketball, the summer was when you worked on improving your range on the jump shot or worked on your left hand dribble or developed better footwork for post play. Getting stronger adding weight or increasing your agility and jumping skills were summer goals to make the high school team a title contender in the winter.

Today the volume of games, exposure, attention, and competition is so abundant that keeping up with what all-star teams you're playing with and when is a daunting task. Often the summer league schedule featuring AAU tournaments is more glamorous than the winter at the local high school. While the athletes seek the new adventures and trips, the solitary practice required for truly improving your weaknesses falls easily by the wayside. It is a shortsighted disservice to the players and their athletic futures.

Think for just one minute–An athlete has been told by his high school coach that next fall he needs to add a left-handed dribble to become the starting point guard. Is that player going to work on the weakness while competing in summer league games against players he knows are just as good or better than he is? Instinctively the player will revert to the strength of his game. In competition the player does not want to lose and definitely does not want to be embarrassed while working on a weakness that he does not have the confidence to execute. Improving on a weakness requires hard, diligent practice and work. This requires passion and true love for the game.

Most youth league programs and teams attended by the athletes in the spring and summer are generally committed to sportsmanship, teaching, and player development, but a growing number seek to win at any cost with the young player caught in the crossfire.

I have watched as nine and ten year old players completely freeze up due to the pressures they encounter during a game. Between vociferous parents screaming for productivity, coaches demanding but not encouraging output, and opponents eager to capitalize on the player's indecisiveness, many youngsters' introduction to the game is bitter and unrewarding. For youth league players, age 10 and under, I believe that scores should not be kept and leagues should be strictly instructional. Player development, sportsmanship, learning and, most importantly, fun should be the priority.

I especially believe this for the sport of basketball because of the skills required to play the game at a competent level. Basketball, with its essential tools of dribbling, passing, and shooting requires an array of techniques and skills that make it different from soccer or tee ball. In these sports, running and pursuit of the ball are the central characteristics. Basketball requires the skill of dribbling and shooting and without the proper teaching or fundamentals it can mentally defeat a player and send him or her away from the game for good. The pace and close quarters of the game ensure every player will eventually have the ball. That is where the excitement begins. It is not a sport played on a big field where you can participate, yet never really be involved. As a youngster, I did not play organized basketball until age 11 or 12. Although my fundamentals might have been lacking, I had an understanding and confidence of the game from playing freely on the playgrounds without pressure and penalty for my mistakes. Through trial and error, I was permitted to fail and ultimately try again. Development is more important than a win at all cost AAU tournament for youth under the age of 10.

Today, this thinking is considered antiquated. Many coaches and league directors say the streets are unsafe and that organized competition is best. Perhaps, but having officiated youth basketball, I believe that a certain level of personal confidence and accomplishment must be gained before a youngster is thrust into an intimidating win now environment. Far too many coaches want to win first and develop youth and sportsmanship later.

Attraction to Addiction: Finding the Proper
Balance with Basketball

I am seeing an adult leadership among coaches and parents that clearly values winning over the merit of teaching, learning, fun and enjoyment for the players. What I have seen up close and personal through officiating is: A) administrators that push the envelop to allow youth to play with age requirements in question. B) Coaches who defiantly ignore the rules regarding the amount of playing time each player on the team must play, usually one full quarter. Some coaches even encourage lesser teammates not to show for the important games such as playoffs to reduce the number of unskilled players he must place in the game. C) Coaches ignore handshake agreements and continue to press full court and pummel undermanned and defeated opponents. This same coach will leave his better players in the game to pad gaudy statistics in blowout games instead of giving playing time to lesser teammates that deserve the opportunity to play. D) Coaches hustle into the game, a star player that arrives late without giving him a proper warm-up. The player replaces a lesser talented player that was on time and working very hard to perform on the court. I think of what lessons are taught here about teamwork, punctuality, and responsibility.

I cringe as nine and ten-year-olds attempt fancy, between the legs dribbling and crossover moves. Their plays are devoid of fundamentals, are blatant rule violations, have the player going nowhere, but do excite roars and catcalls from the stands. As a referee, I immediately call traveling or carrying the ball violations. Meanwhile, the coach wants to chastise me instead of the cartoon antics of his player. Worse yet, I abhor the grandstanding coach who verbally abuses the officials and sometimes his players with unnecessary theatrics. I recall listening to a coach confront a nine-year old player during a game and yell to the athlete, "If you don't start playing better it will be your fault that the team won't go to Disney World [to compete in a national AAU tournament]."

When I encounter a youth league coach that I see consumed with winning a ball game, I seek confrontation during the game with him. His priorities are obviously compromised. The game is about his ego and personal gratification and no longer about the athletes. I hold these coaches accountable. The young players feed off his emotions. If the coach becomes animated, emotional, and upset with the officials or opposing players you can believe his nine- and ten-year-old players will respond accordingly. The coach is there for leadership, adult supervision, teaching of fundamentals and sportsmanship, and to provide a positive role model image. Youth league sports of all ages and especially under the age of 11 should highlight these attributes.

Meanwhile, under the bright lights of basketball there seems to be no way young athletes can keep their perspective and keep their athletic accomplishments in balance with the rest of their lives. With so many parameters outside of their control youth, and particularly Black youth in the big city, get swept away toward selling out their innocence, their intelligence, their imagination, their expectations and their options to play the game of basketball. What starts as an attraction at such a young age quickly degenerates into an addiction that will ultimately be a hard fought battle to keep basketball in a proper perspective. With understanding, vision and a reevaluation of goals, the game of basketball can be used for enormous growth and promise instead of the reverse where the game uses the player. However, with each new season that goal seems to be fleeing.

Another more subtle measure leading Black youth to an addictive relationship to basketball is the preponderance of successful Black athletes in basketball and football in the college and professional ranks. With television highlighting this fact almost every night, its impact on both the Black and White athlete is a topic for inspection. In fact subliminal messages in televised sports have altered the mental outlook on sports of both Black and White athlete albeit in different ways.

The Black athlete watches college and professional basketball and, to a lesser degree, football, and takes an inventory of the large numbers of Black players participating and excelling in the sports. These athletes become immediate role models and are imitated by most young athletes. Black youth, already raised on sports idolatry, see the sheer numbers of athletic players and stars and believe that sports success is their imperial and designated right. All other career pursuits pale by comparison. It is an easy sell to convince the Black youth that sports will be their success.

Meanwhile, the White athlete, it appears, has all but conceded his role in basketball and football to the Black athlete. Contrary to the Black athlete, the White athlete does not see as many role models in basketball and football and accepts the premise that the Black athlete, whether out of desire, physiology, economics, etc., is the better player in these sports. The absence or declining role of the White athlete in football and basketball seems to be comparable to when the Black community did not see Black professionals in corporate America in the '50s and '60s. Sometimes, the White athlete does not even bother to compete in these sports assuming it to be "a Black sport" and bypasses participation for spectator glorification. As I have officiated basketball games in suburban communities over the last 17 years, it has always amazed me when high schools that have White student enrollment of 70 percent or greater field basketball teams that have a majority of Black athletes.

This is not a positive situation. First, Black athletes begin to feel a measure of athletic superiority and entitlement that is counterproductive to their self-esteem and total development as a person. They are also allowing themselves to be forced into a certain path that highlights physical attributes while alternately ignoring their mental and intellectual capabilities. Also, the adulation that accompanies sports and the expansion of Black athletic domination of college and professional basketball is watched every night by Black youth and a belief is established that sports presents them with a guarantee of success. This becomes a false sense of security and only perpetuates the dream of a professional athletic career.

Meanwhile, the White athlete's willingness to forfeit athletic participation in basketball and football to the Black athlete encourages more and lesser talented Black athletes to try out for these sports teams and fall into the same funnel of athletic addiction.

I have interviewed and questioned many administrators, teachers, and parents at these schools about the disparity between Black and White athletic participation and school enrollment. Many Whites say they don't see it as an issue. They believe that it is a natural occurrence without any serious ramifications. It seems as if they subconsciously believe that sports participation, at least basketball and football, are supposed to be played by the Black athlete.

Many Black parents, administrators, and sports personnel seem to agree but are forthright in proudly saying that the issue is simply because the Black athlete is better. However, a Black golf coach at a school in Prince George's County provided an enlightening perspective. He said that it is a serious problem and that sports participation is clearly nothing more than athletic segregation. The coach added, "Black athletes apparently have dominion over basketball and the skill positions of football while White athletes have the same over sports of lacrosse and golf. Every year despite over 800 Black kids in the school maybe, with luck, one or two Black athletes try out for the golf team. It's cultural and now more than ever comfortably accepted by high school students."

I have watched too many examples of Black athletes playing basketball at predominately White schools while the White students are content to just cheer. Howard High School in the affluent suburb of Columbia, Maryland has a White enrollment of 70-75 percent and fielded a basketball team of approximately 12 Black athletes on its 13 or 14 player roster. The team did not have any players over 6'2." The players were not very skilled or talented and I doubt that any player on the team would earn a basketball scholarship to college.

Attraction to Addiction: Finding the Proper Balance with Basketball

There is absolutely no way that a school with 1500 students did not have any White athletes that were more talented than the Black athletes on the team. The White athletes apparently chose not to play and would rather be spectators.

It is a very interesting dynamic how the White community can concede sports participation to Black basketball players. At another game in Columbia held at Centennial High School which is approximately 80-85 percent White, a good-sized, mostly White crowd watched their teams, go through the 20 minute pre-game drills while listening to the loud, thunderous, rhythm of Black hip-hop music blaring from the gymnasium speakers. It was a very interesting sociological statement. Perhaps the White community is right that sports participation by Black and White athletes is not a big issue. Just like listening to rap music before a game, the White community is only concerned with entertainment and sports enjoyment. They have financial options and privilege, exposure, confidence and connections to pursue any venue in our society. The long term, hooked on hoops complications of single-minded, low expectation, Black athletes is not their concern.

CHAPTER SEVEN
Our Black Athletes Are Future Kings

It is not an easy task for Black athletes. The pathway to the courts is loaded with minefields. For surviving the pitfalls of his surroundings he should be commended and know that a future king is among us, not because of his basketball talent but for his instincts and intelligence. Unfortunately, it is the athletic talent displayed on the court that is roundly applauded while his struggle to get to the court is downplayed or even ignored. It should not be this way.

The Black athlete must be street-wise and smart enough to distance himself from drugs in the neighborhood as well as inside the school. I remember a conversation prior to a varsity game I was refereeing at Lincoln Junior High School in Washington DC, where Cardozo High School of northwest DC was to play Ballou High School from southeast. I had a discussion with the respective head coaches of the schools, Henry Lindsay at Cardozo and Wanda Oates of Ballou, about why their teams as well as other teams in the Washington area public schools lacked tall and big players. Many teams lacked players over 6'5 and I had officiated a great number of games featuring 6'3" centers and 6'2" power forwards. I asked the coaches, "Are teams devoid of tall players? My high school team at St. Anthony's featured 7 players over 6'4." Is this just my imagination or a reality?"

Without hesitation both coaches responded that big athletes are still around. In fact, they walk the halls at school. They are probably apathetic toward the game. It is likely they are more content to become drug lieutenants and enforcers for gangs and drugs than to set their sights on a future in the game. The coaches concluded that the fast life and the quick buck had changed the environment so that sports no longer held their interests and the dollar was far more attractive than having to work hard on the court and in the classroom.

An assistant coach formely at a Prince George's County public school that won a Maryland state championship told me that there are plenty of Black males that can play basketball and want to play basketball but can't or do not want to make the commitment to leave their activities, associates, and habits of the streets. The coach said he personally went into the tough neighborhoods to recruit talented players. To get the All-Metropolitan star of the championship team the assistant coach said he made a "deal" with the athlete. The assistant coach told the young man if he would come to class, forgo using drugs and running with his "boys" during the week he would not ask any questions about what the player did on the weekends. It worked. The team won. The talented athlete stayed out of trouble and went on to play college basketball.

Obviously, it is not that easy. The Black athlete must first separate himself from the drug culture and its temptation to provide a fast dollar and addictive habit. Extracting himself from the drug scene is probably the most dangerous and devastating pitfall the Black athlete must overcome. The drug culture is omnipresent. A former coach at a high school in southeast Washington DC confided to me just how pervasive the drug scene is and how it should never be underestimated.

While preparing for a game against another city school, the coach and his assistants always have their players place their clothing and belongings in a huge canvas zippered ball bag. The bag is then taken to the court and placed in the team bench area. This is done as a safety precaution against theft. After the game, the coach gathers all the uniforms for washing and takes the canvas bag home. On one particular night, while washing the uniforms, the coach noticed his two-year-old son playing with a plastic pouch filled with leaves. It was a one-pound bag of marijuana that obviously had fallen from the pockets of one of his players. After his immediate concern that his son did not ingest any of the drugs, the coach became irate with his team.

Our Black Athletes Are Future Kings

While having an idea of which player was responsible, but unable to prove it, the coach addressed the team in a meeting the next day. He told the players bluntly and forcefully that if he had the slightest inkling or suspicion of any drug activity by any player he would cancel the rest of the season. The drug scene and its severe implications is just one of many dangerous impediments faced by the Black athlete.

The Black athlete must overcome poor conditions in the schools including overcrowded classrooms, deteriorating buildings, and overworked guidance counselors with unmanageable student ratios. School buildings have leaky roofs inadequate heat in the winter, poor ventilation in the summer and no running water in the bathrooms and water fountains. The lack of useable text books, toilet paper, and functional computers is often the rule rather than the exception. Most damaging of all are the many apathetic teachers that have low to no expectations for the students personally and academically.

I vividly remember a discussion with a basketball athlete at a Prince George's County school. I had asked the young man why when the report cards came out in February so many of his teammates had failing grades and therefore were dismissed from the team. His reply was confusing yet illuminating. "The teachers make it easy for us to fail. They don't expect nothing from us and that is what a lot of the players do—nothing." The unhealthy teacher-student relationship is reflected in the poor graduation rates of predominately Black youth. Washington DC officials reported that one out of every three students who entered the ninth grade drops out of school.

Meanwhile, our Black athlete has managed to dodge street violence, by no means an easy task, where the slightest altercation or misunderstanding can lead to retribution with guns. Incidents that can occur at what are presumed to be the most innocent of public ventures—a free concert in the park, a sale at a sporting goods store in the mall or just a date with your girlfriend at a movie—have our male youth questioning just what is a "safe" activity. For athletes to stay clear of school and neighborhood feuds is a tough proposition.

A coach at a public school in Washington DC told me how one of his star players did not want to seem like a "punk" if he didn't support his boys "beefin" with another group. The athlete said it was a "pride" and "manhood" situation. After considerable urging from the coach, including telling the athlete "that he would end up as just another Black kid killed on the corner without anyone giving a damn," the athlete changed his mind.

I personally remember a high school game I officiated where an All-City player from Dunbar High, aware that college scouts were in the gym to see him, scored 22 points in the first half of a game against a cross-city rival school. Early in the third quarter the player retaliated after an opposing player hit him with a punch. Both players were ejected from the game. Later that summer I gave the athlete a ride home after an all-star practice. As we discussed the incident, the young man told me that the following day after the game he got a ride to the rival school and fought the same player again off campus at a lunch time deli. When I asked the athlete why, he said, "The guy sucker-punched me and could have messed up my chance for a scholarship." The athlete did sign with a Division I university.

Our Black athlete has been able to avoid trouble with the law and a possible rap sheet. Again this is not an easy endeavor with the attack and harassment of Black youth (especially Black males) by police and law enforcement officials that seem to exalt in locking up Black youth and asking questions later. Police harassment towards Blacks in neighboring Prince George's and Montgomery Counties in Maryland is documented and legendary. Black youth know to tread wisely and in numbers for safety in case of a confrontation not with rival youths but with police. In Prince George's

Our Black Athletes Are Future Kings

County an increase in incidents between police using excessive force against the community, especially Black male youth, has forced some Black churches to have seminars and forums to raise the awareness of the citizenry on how to protect themselves in an encounter with the law.

Often our Black athletes come from dysfunctional families with multiple and fractious problems. Many times young boys are thrust into the position of "man of the house" in their middle or early teens and must oversee the care of younger brothers and sisters. It can lead to a very unsettling, intimidating, and unsure time. In Washington DC, many women's sports in high schools such as softball and track & field are cancelled because young ladies need to stay at home or work part time to provide for younger siblings. Even in basketball some coaches do not schedule games on weekends because many of their female players would not be able to attend the games because of family concerns or jobs. Often coaches have allowed their female players to bring younger siblings with them to games and bus trips because no other provisions are available. All of these circumstances are shoved on the young Black athlete as he or she must also deal with the pain and psychological impact of poverty and while often going without the essentials in life that most people take for granted.

Athletically, our Black athletes must stay free from career-threatening injuries despite playing basketball almost year round without significant and necessary rest periods. Today, he must travel to camps, summer leagues and AAU tournaments usually in order for some other adult or program to prosper such as a shoe company, AAU coach/program or tournament director. Most are using the athlete's name to increase attendance and value for a given venue. Consequently, the athlete must always have his "A-game" because other players will either want to challenge him or, in the case of some bitter and jealous athletes, may want to hurt him.

At one of these elite showcase tournaments held at the aptly named Showplace Arena in Prince George's County, Lamar Odom, considered the top high school basketball player in the nation in 1996-97, played against Cardozo High School from Washington DC. With the outcome of the game no longer in doubt a couple of the players on the defeated and frustrated Cardozo team clearly, and with malicious intent, hit Odom with hard and purposeful fouls. As their coach quickly pulled the players out of the game, they were delighted with themselves for the shots they took at the NBA bound Odom.

Yet with all this activity in the life of our Black athlete in order to accept a college scholarship and be immediately eligible to play he has to manage to have the necessary grade point average and satisfactory score on the culturally if not racially biased Scholastic Assessment Test (SAT). Truly, our Black athletes, men and women, are soldiers and warriors for what they have to endure at such a young age before even deciding on a college to attend. Yet, armed with exceptional athletic skills our Black athletes keep on marching for a better day. Often it is their belief in their basketball skills combined with having a dream of reaching a professional basketball career that keeps them focused and mentally strong enough to rise above their turbulent environment.

CHAPTER EIGHT:
Private High School Recruiting

Two primary culprits that inflate Black youths' sense of self-worth through basketball are the recruiting by private schools and the impact of the AAU. It has long been one of the worst kept secrets in scholastic sports that private schools recruit athletes and provide scholarships for them to attend their schools. Only now, in the beginning of the new millennium have the private schools sheepishly gone public with this revelation. Still they attempt to soften their plea, wanting everyone to understand that recruiting is solely for the purpose of enhancing declining enrollments. Private school administrators say recruiting athletes is not any different than trying to attract outstanding academic students.

Private schools work very hard to recruit young athletes as early as the sixth grade. Many of the tactics used would make college recruiters blush. With the backing of sneaker companies, the benefits and features of the private schools far outdistance what the public schools offer. Private school recruiting is a slick business and often has helped develop a youth sports subculture of selfish, pampered athletes with oversized egos. The recruiting of middle school athletes and younger has manufactured an athlete devoid of loyalty, with an exaggerated, fantasy life relationship with basketball.

The problem is especially keen for the Black athlete. Black youth raised poor without much positive re-enforcement are easy prey to the sales pitch of recruiters. Predominately, White men heap praise on parents over their son's potential physical gifts, while also speaking of the advantages of a private school education. Immediately dreams of sports headlines, all-city honors, and scholarship offers from all the famous major college basketball powers take flight. Caution and wise decision-making are needed, but instead are replaced by visions of NBA stardom.

Many parents lose perspective. If Black parents are four times more likely than White parents to believe that their children will have a professional career in sports, what chance does a 13 year old have of staying levelheaded while he is the subject of a recruiting battle for his athletic talents among a half dozen schools?

For many athletes, dreams do come true. A private school education and athletic career can be a strong foundation for becoming a successful athlete and citizen. Hopefully, the student athlete is rewarded with a college scholarship, graduation from college (which should be the ultimate goal) and possibly a professional sports opportunity. However, parents must see the whole picture. Attending a private school solely for its athletic program negates their academic and social responsibility. Many parents and athletes fail to realize this and it can neutralize athletic success. Athletes often develop a nomadic lifestyle as they jump from high school to high school and college to college searching for the NBA dream.

One of the saddest things to observe is an athlete bouncing from several junior high and high schools because he thinks he will be a star. When private schools come calling, it is a very hard sell to tell a family living in poverty not to jump at the opportunity. They give assurances that tuition will be "handled by the school." The reality is there are no guarantees. Many of these schools recruit the best players nationwide each year. The fine print of the scholarship says renewal is contingent upon your performance. How can you perform when your playing time has been drastically reduced? There are no four year scholarships. Many parents pay the tuition in hopes of future college and NBA possibilities.

So, when a representative or coach from a private school has a "happenstance" conversation with a young athlete it is not time for celebration because you have reached the yellow brick road to athletic stardom. If anything, it could be the brick road to a hard realization of what sports and competition are like with the "big boys." It can be an eye-opening experience and a preview of what life will be about after his days of basketball are finished and he must compete daily in the workplace to provide for his family.

Private High School Recruiting

For Black youth this is not necessarily bad. After all, life after sports will not be easy and you will have to compete the rest of your life under unfair conditions. The question becomes for the parent, is this the lesson you want for your child at this age? Black parents in particular need to understand that sending their youth to the highly visible, tradition-laden, nationally ranked private school will place their son in a season-to-season competition with no promises, guarantees, loyalty, or security.

Prominent programs that seem to compete on the national high school basketball level year in and year out include St. Anthony of Jersey City, New Jersey; Rice, Christ the King, and St. Raymond from New York City and state; Roman Catholic in Philadelphia; Country Day near Detroit; St. Julian in Chicago and Mater Dei in California. These programs and others generally produce successful teams, have excellent coaching and adult leadership, and send tremendously gifted athletes to our top colleges. But the commitment to stay on top and win is very intense and competitive and these schools usually have an overabundance of aspiring athletes wanting to enroll and play basketball. Often unsuspecting, hooked on hoops parents and athletes fail to understand the scope and competitiveness of these programs.

Almost every large city has a private high school basketball powerhouse. In the Washington area, legendary DeMatha Catholic High School in Hyattsville, Maryland is renowned as one of the greatest basketball schools in this country. Hall of Fame coach Morgan Wooten has won more basketball games than any other high school coach in the nation. More importantly, Morgan Wooten and the DeMatha program have possibly sent more athletes to play college basketball than any other high school in the country. DeMatha is the prototype for private institutions.

A prime example of the national scope of the DeMatha program is illustrated in Joe Forte, a tremendous guard-forward and High School All-American. Forte was a basketball legend in Georgia.

His mother, concerned that her son was losing perspective, called Morgan Wooten and asked if the talented player could come to DeMatha. Wooten, like any other high school coach readily accepted the gifted athlete who probably could have started on any team in the nation. The arrival of Forte and his brother, Jason, meant that two positions currently held by players within the program would have to be vacated for the new additions. Yet, DeMatha need not apologize to anyone. Sport is competition. Life is competition. There are no promises. Parents and young players need to realize that as a nationally recognized program DeMatha's pool of potential athletes is greater than most. Productivity is the priority. While the Forte story is indeed a rare occurrence, recruiting is a constant at the big time private school programs and good players and their families are constantly seeking out the brightest spotlight for their talents. Parents need to understand the energy and scope of big time private school basketball. If parents fail to grasp the concept they should not cry if athletic success does not touch their athlete at the private school.

After high school, All-American stars like Forte continue to keep the private school tradition and name in front of the sports community. After his high school career, Forte accepted a scholarship to the University of North Carolina. His high school teammate Keith Bogans, also a high school All-American, accepted a scholarship to the University of Kentucky. Both men started as freshmen and were among their team's leading scorers, respectively. Their highly regarded teams were constantly on national television. Announcers and commentators often recited their DeMatha backgrounds several times during the course of a game. Can you think of any better advertisement or recruitment tool for the DeMatha program to young basketball players and their parents than the immediate success of these two standout performers? It is very easy to visualize young athletes, after watching Forte and Bogans, telling their parents how they want to go to DeMatha Catholic High School.

Private High School Recruiting

Over the last 15 years, I have officiated many DeMatha Varsity basketball games and also worked Junior Varsity and Freshman games. I was disturbed to see pre-game lay-up lines with as many as sixteen players for each DeMatha team. Both teams were tall and athletic. Clearly, the athletes were committed and talented. Almost always, they would blow out some hapless foe. But that is not the issue. It is impossible for 32 freshman and sophomore players to all move up to the varsity level. Each season the varsity probably loses only about five players; toss into the mix transfer athletes from other schools that will play varsity immediately (like Forte) and the available varsity roster spots are again reduced. The sheer numbers say most will either transfer or quit the sport.

I spoke to many parents in the stands. They make great sacrifices to have their children attend DeMatha. These parents, both Black and White, make huge commitments regarding tuition costs and usually travel great distances from their homes to accommodate practice and game schedules. They get off work to diligently attend games. These parents mention with pride how the DeMatha coaching staff has said their athlete has potential to help the program. Clearly, they are committed to their young athletes and they join their sons in the promise of a bright athletic future. I give a gracious nod of encouragement and offer good luck but I know that a good percentage of the players are in over their heads. Parents just do not seem to understand the level of competition at schools like DeMatha. Their JV teams can go out and play a full schedule against some varsity teams, and when the dust settles, will have a winning record. Their teams are that strong.

Recruiting is always a priority. During the Christmas break, DeMatha hosts a 54-team youth basketball tournament. The tournament is held in the DeMatha gymnasium and is hailed as a community service and outreach program. It is also a local recruiting vehicle providing DeMatha with a big advantage. The rival schools in the area simply cannot compete against this venue. DeMatha literature and brochures are given freely to over 500 twelve to fourteen year old basketball players plus coaches and parents during the course of the tournament. Impromptu conversations occur and praise is given to athletes by DeMatha coaches and personnel. Athletes bask in the glow of playing on the same floor where all the great DeMatha stars of the past played and practiced. More phone numbers, business cards, and handshakes are given than at a Chamber of Commerce business luncheon. Youngsters return home and immediately tell their parents that DeMatha is where they want to attend while rationalizing how it would be beneath their abilities to attend their neighborhood public school. For emphasis youngsters mention how a DeMatha coach cited that they were a "good looking athlete." You would be surprised at how many Black parents take the bait and begin the process of seeing if they can somehow incorporate the DeMatha tuition into their budget.

The coaches and administrators at DeMatha distinctly understand that winning and increased enrollments are their primary obligations, and they pursue these tasks with the passion of car salesmen seeking a monthly bonus for exceeding quota. They understand that attrition is part of the selection process. They know that when the smoke clears the better athletes will surface and the program can remain strong.

DeMatha does not owe anyone—parents, players, or rivals—any explanation. They are in the sports business to win. Their "only the strong survive" approach to high school basketball works for them. Many private schools that are harsh critics of DeMatha's style secretly admire their way of doing business. DeMatha is the envy of and prototype for other private schools that want successful and winning basketball programs.

Meanwhile, Black parents hooked on hoops can't fault DeMatha if their athlete can't survive the program. Parents should have done their homework before enrollment. Black parents should not send their athletes to a private school without first taking a hard look at their own motivations.

Private High School Recruiting

In thirty years of basketball involvement, I believe that the Black family's infatuation with attending elite private schools has damaged the careers of more young Black athletes than it has aided. Both Black youth and parents are naïve to the intensity, pressure and calculated cold business decisions that are made regarding private school basketball programs. Yet, the high visibility, self-satisfied, above the fray, king-of-the-hill reputation, and status one is afforded in the Black community for allegedly making it to the top forces them to lose perspective.

Black parents need to understand that paying tuition or receiving financial assistance from the school does not give them or the athlete rewards or advantages. If the potential of the young athlete is not reached and reached quickly he will be replaced, period. No questions asked. For Black families who are hooked on hoops, this can be especially painful because the fall from anticipated stardom impacts so many different areas—social, academic, athletic, psychological, and financial. Black parents too easily blame the whole episode on the system or coach. They do not perform an honest analysis of their athlete's skills. Parents who want a scholarship for their youth unconsciously or intentionally place pressure on their children. Suddenly, a young Black athlete with abundant potential feels like the weight of the world is on his back. His high school innocence is replaced with the reality of basketball as a business venture. The Black athlete first and foremost wants to play basketball. His identity and self worth are tied to the sport. He feels his best chance to attend college is through basketball, not academics or his family's savings. This started with a lack of understanding of the severity of basketball recruiting at the big time private school.

Conversely, when athletics turns sour for White families they usually have multiple choices in reserve. They have the income to choose another private school or their athlete can attend the local public school. Usually the public school is in an upstanding suburban neighborhood and is a safe, well-equipped environment, offering an outstanding academic curriculum with a high percentage of its students moving onto higher education. For the White family, the athlete can forgo sports participation altogether, maintain his respect from his peer and attend college through academic achievement or family financial status. The White community does not place its athletes on the same pedestal and under as bright a spotlight as the Black community. Therefore, walking away from the game or competing on a local boys club level is not perceived as a failure.

Black parents say, and probably do think, they are sending their son to a private school for the right reasons. True, they value the athletic program, but they are cognizant of advantages private schools have over public schools. They highlight the importance of school safety, smaller classroom size, fewer, if any, "problem kids" and one-on-one tutoring. Academic standards are lofty and a high percentage of the students advance to higher education, usually with scholarships. Facilities and supplies are better. Rules and regulations are enforced.

For most families, the reasons are valid for seeking a private school education for their child. However, parents must take a critical look to locate the best opportunity for their son to play basketball and they must make the decision based on the best interest of their child. Many parents that have the financial ability to send their child to private school automatically assume that upon paying the tuition all is well. The child is in a safe, progressive environment that is conducive to his academic and athletic growth. The thought process sounds accurate. But if basketball is truly the primary motivator and the number one reason why a private school was chosen then all the other reasons are truly secondary. The athlete would stay and complete high school and not transfer if basketball were eliminated. Basketball is the catalyst for everything else at the school. If the young man is producing athletically then academically he is likely to do well. If the reverse happens and basketball is a struggle then the athlete will have difficulty in the classroom. All of which can lead to transferring and the nomadic high school lifestyle.

Private High School Recruiting

To avoid this dilemma, parents must evaluate the selection of a private school with the same level of research required to buy a house, select a doctor, or accept a new job. Parents that have to handle tuition need to understand that these private institutions want your child to enroll. Many private schools have declining enrollments and they need your child. Consequently, you are the client and the private school should fulfill your needs instead of the reverse. If your child is a talented athlete, it can increase your choices of schools.

Take your time. Be selective. Interview the personnel, including the principal, coach, athletic director, and academic coordinators. Ask about the racial composition of the faculty, administration, and student body. If they are predominately White but the team is primarily Black, then winning basketball games is the school's priority. Ask the coach for a list of Black players and their phone numbers who have gone to college within five years. Ask to speak to current players and parents. Interview the athletic director separately from the coach; sometimes their visions are different. This should be done for every school considered. It's hard and exhausting, but essential. Parents need to remember that they have the upper hand. The schools want your son's talent, your money or both.

Scholarship parents need to proceed more cautiously than tuition-paying parents. They need to understand that they are entering into an employee-employer relationship that will be re-evaluated each year. It is not a four-year commitment. Their child must produce athletically or there will be serious consequences. Bad grades, a bad attitude, and bad games eliminate scholarships. Heaven forbid a serious injury. What once appeared to be a dream come true can rapidly dissipate into a nightmare for parent and athlete. I recommend that parents seek legal counsel to review any documents before signing. If they cannot afford a lawyer seek a paralegal. Many churches and social service agencies can provide free or inexpensive legal counsel.

Buyer Beware! There are plenty of private schools to choose from and most have excellent academic programs. However, if basketball exposure and the level of competition are higher priorities than learning and academic success then parents need to proceed with caution. There are a lot of private schools that flash on and off the radar of top-level high school basketball. Often these schools make a brief splash, coming out of obscurity to occasionally jockey for city rankings. It is a fleeting stay among the elite teams in the city and the notoriety is short-lived. In essence, what you end up seeing is a good team every now and then, but not necessarily a good athletic program. This distinction between program and team is very important. If it is not a program that has made the commitment to stay in big time athletics, parents are setting themselves and their athlete up for a frustrating and temporary stay at the school, while purchasing a ticket to a nomadic high school career.

There are many reasons why most private schools have a momentary period of success in basketball. The most obvious reason is a flawed athletic vision. The philosophy of many private schools is, "lets put up a couple of rims and backboards and find some Black boys to play." It is a harsh reality, but it is the quickest way for small private schools to increase enrollment, gain notoriety, and substantially improve cash flow. A competitive basketball program is a very cost effective venture. It does not require a major investment in relation to other sports like football. Basketball with its position of prominence in the Black community, is also the quickest way for a private school to recruit athletes and gain exposure within the city or surrounding suburbs.

It would take a naïve person to think that money can't be made off the backs and efforts of Black youth. The same philosophy used by the colleges and universities applies to high school athletics. Most private schools receive their recognition within the game of basketbal through the substantial efforts and labor of Black athletes. The truth of the matter is that a private school education is not a panacea for the Black athlete. Some of these private schools are reaching and grasping to balance their budgets, increase their enrollments and seek acclaim and prominence. Many of these private schools envision themselves as another DeMatha high school basketball powerhouse. In this haste to achieve DeMatha-like status many Black families get chewed up in the process. St. Vincent Pallotti High School in Laurel, Maryland envisioned itself as capable of challenging DeMatha. But Pallotti, in its zeal to contend with the big boys, left a trail of frustrated athletes and upset and betrayed parents. In six years under Coach Mike Glick, approximately 40 athletes, mostly Black, transferred from the school. Many of the players never even made the varsity roster. The athletes and concerned parents were pawns for Glick to get an established program that in turn would help him secure a college coaching position. Eventually, Glick left the head coaching position and Pallotti has scaled back its basketball program and projection.

I have officiated private school basketball games from southern Prince George's County to affluent Montgomery County in Maryland to flourishing Fairfax County, Virgina and through the bustling big cities of Alexandria and Arlington, Virginia and Washington DC. I have seen many of these same private schools go from perennial contenders to total elimination of their athletic programs. As I went to the gymnasiums of these private schools to referee, I was aware that their basketball programs often shared many of the same goals and problems. For example, the gyms were woefully small and not ready for big time basketball. Capacity seating was approximately 200 spectators or less at many of these gyms and the facilities were second rate. Visiting teams and referees had to change in classrooms or hallway bathrooms. Parking was inadequate an indication that the school was not ready for the influx of cars and traffic into the community to follow a highly visible winning team. The school would not be able to accommodate or handle the increased fan attention and would cause a burden to the surrounding neighborhoods.

Probably the greatest demonstration of a program doing a total disservice to its athletes was a game I officiated involving private school basketball powers, Laurel Baptist and St. Johns Prospect Hall. The game was a home date for Laurel Baptist and they played their games at Laurel Boys and Girls club, a facility over 75 years old and barely adequate for a Catholic Youth Organization (CYO) championship game. Laurel Baptist featured high school All-American Louis Bullock, who later starred for the University of Michigan. St Johns Prospect Hall was ranked #5 by *USA Today*. They had several talented major college athletes highlighted by All-American, and eventual Duke University signee, Nate James.

The game should have been played at a local community college with a large regulation size floor and seating for a couple of thousand spectators. Instead the gym had a capacity of about 200 or less spectators and was jammed packed. The school probably lost more money at the door turning away spectators than they made by selling tickets. The floor was at a minimum twenty feet shorter than regulation length for high school basketball. There was only about one yard of space between the spectators and the sidelines of the floor making safety an issue for fans, players, and referees.

Regardless, the game played on and the athletes adjusted as always. Laurel Baptist upset the bigger and talented Prospect Hall team. The overriding factor in the game was the familiarity of the gym to the home team. Bullock, a tremendous shooter, especially from three-point range, scored 40 points in the game. Many of his shots came as he took just a couple of steps across half court. Stunned Prospect Hall defenders did not consider defending a shot from that distance, and never adjusted its zone defense to contest a shot from that range. But the shot was not a half court heave and in actuality, it was no more than 35 feet from the basket—still a long distance shot, but a shot Bullock could hit. Considering the magnitude of the game, the high caliber of athletes competing, and the potential for a large crowd, planning for the contest was shortsighted and incomplete. Ironically, five years later, neither school competes on the top level of high school basketball in the Washington D.C. area.

The communities surrounding private schools that wish to have a big time basketball team must be in agreement over the goals for a better athletic program. It is the local community that has supported the school through the enrollment of their children and community activities. A problem occurs if the local community feels that their own youngsters and neighborhood projects will become secondary to basketball.

Many of the private schools located in the suburbs experience resistance when, all of a sudden, the local community is faced with Black athletes attending their schools and taking playing opportunities away from their children. Often, this is a major source of conflict between the community and the school. There is resentment over Black athletes coming into their neighborhoods. Private schools often create segregation due to tuition. Forced busing was one thing, but now paying Black athletes to play a game is a different matter altogether.

Another point of contention is the faculty and administrators within the school. They realize the influx of Black athletes create a clashing of cultures and socio-economic differences. There is resentment over Black athletes attending the school tuition free just to play basketball. Many private schools think basketball would be the answer to their woes, but instead presents a multitude of problems never before considered. The ill-conceived premise of becoming a high school sports power is not as easy as purchasing new uniforms and scheduling a home game with DeMatha.

Concessions and compromises had to be made on several different levels. Academic standards and teaching techniques needed to be reassessed because many of the athletes were coming from schools where standards and expectations were very low. These student-athletes required individual attention in order to stay eligible to play basketball.

113

I know of several private schools where athletes were accepted without their academic transcripts ever being reviewed. One private school in Southern Prince George's county accepted athletes regardless of how dismal their academic record. The school's attitude is to forgive past academic sins. The athlete enters the school with a clean slate. While a second chance is commendable, what system is in place to actually assist the youngster? Would the second chance be forthcoming if not for an ability to make jump shots? What happens to the athlete if his shooting percentage is 25 percent?

Private schools that want a big time sports program find that they must make concessions on religion. Many of the athletes do not have the same spiritual beliefs and have different religious denominations. While respectful of the schools' religious practices and traditions, many athletes do not have a desire to learn or understand theology. Religious practices and traditions are viewed as "a free period" from the normal school routine.

At St. Anthony's High School, I and many of my teammates were not Catholic. On occasions when class was suspended for mass or church services it was merely an opportunity to secretly "cut up" with your buddies from other classes. Religion class could just as easily have been Latin or college trigonometry. We failed to see its relevance and treated the subject with disdain.

Due to the suburban locations of many of the private schools, boarding accommodations needed to be made for some athletes. Many of these athletes were without transportation. To ensure the recruited athlete would make it to class, practice, and games, schools had to consider housing. Many coaches have taken athletes into their homes for the school year. Have the same coaches ever taken into their homes academic Black students?

Social considerations had to be addressed. For example, perhaps unaware of their respective Black and White cultures a disagreement occurs between a Black ballplayer and White student. When the situation is brought to the school administration it is deemed a misunderstanding. Yet, the school has strict disciplinary rules regarding fighting. Does the school compromise their rules? Change rules? Make an exception?

Another issue is dating. While many private schools have exclusive enrollments of either all boys or girls, some have coed populations. The issue has to at least be addressed, because Black athletes attending all White schools will eventually date White girls from the school, sister school, or surrounding neighborhoods. This can lead to friction within the school and community.

While misjudging the impact of the surrounding community is the primary off the court reason for the turnover of private school basketball programs, the other part of the equation is a failure to understand the intensity and scope of recruiting athletes. High school basketball in the Black community has its own sub-culture. Many private schools do not have a grasp of this concept. Fielding a high caliber team each season requires a commitment to roll up the shirtsleeves and get down and dirty in the recruiting process for athletes.

Unfortunately, today that requires snuggling up to the AAU programs. It also requires a year round commitment of time and energy and money. It requires networking, phone calls, home visits, and scouting boys clubs middle school programs and games. It requires striking up relationships with untrustworthy people and others that are out for profit instead of the welfare of young athletes. In the Black community, high school basketball is now a 12-month proposition. It is no longer just a winter sport activity.

Game schedules for private school basketball teams are one way to attract players and are a distinct advantage over public schools. Private schools can pretty much do what they want with their athletic programs in comparison to public schools. They can start their season before and end their season after public schools. They are not restricted by distance and, most important, how many games they can play. Many private schools believe that bigger is better, and more games equal more revenue and exposure.

Consequently, it is commonplace to see private schools playing a schedule exceeding 35 games. Clearly, it is a portrait of a program chasing money, notoriety, exposure, and big time athletic success. It is also a clear indictment of a program that is exploiting primarily Black athletes athletically and academically.

It is very apparent that a private school basketball team that plays 35 or more games does not have a serious concern for the academic interests of its athletes. The lack of academic priorities becomes a great disservice to the athletes. They receive interest from colleges from playing this inflated schedule, but since they do not have the grades or SAT exam scores to qualify, many of the universities do not offer them an athletic scholarship.

Parents need to be razor sharp regarding this issue. If college is the major goal don't let basketball destroy it. A 35 to 45 game schedule requires a tremendous amount of time spent away from the classroom. Some games require overnight or weekend stays. Several games can involve plane trips and missing a full week of classes. There is absolutely no way that academic success is achieved with this type of schedule. In comparison, public schools in Maryland can only play 22 games (not including county and state playoffs.) The season starts the first week in December and ends in late February. Even the NCAA allows its member institutions to schedule just 28 games independent of tournaments. The college schedule runs from the first week of November through March, including tournaments.

Therefore, if the NCAA allows its colleges 28 games and most states permit their high schools a 22 game schedule, how can a private school justify a 35-40 game schedule and say it is concerned about the academic interest of the student athletes? The NCAA and the respective state governing bodies for high schools did not arbitrarily pick the number of games out of a hat. While other considerations such as state budgets were part of the selection process, time spent away from the classroom was certainly a high priority. Apparently, private schools with 35 or more games feel the decision-making process of these agencies is flawed and unacceptable. Yet, the logic about missed class time is evident. For every game played consider it one less day of academics.

At St. Anthony's High School, classroom assignments and homework were an afterthought on game days. We were too hyped about the game to concentrate in class. Our focus was on our opponent and what we needed to do to win. If the game featured local stars, friends, or playground rivals it would only increase our anxiousness. The day was usually spent clock-watching and trying to stay out of trouble with teachers to avoid being disciplined by our coach.

Many times on game days, the bus leaves the school before classes are dismissed. In most schools, JV plays before the Varsity team and for budget and convenience reasons both teams travel together. Therefore, getting to an evening game against a cross-town rival for two games is the start of a long night. The games may not conclude until 9:30 and after a return trip to the school many players do not get home until close to 11:00. In all likelihood, homework will not happen. Clearly, studies are not high on the athlete's to-do list. The athlete replays the game and his performance, and attempts to sleep. The bottom line is that a day of study is easily lost when there is a game for the athlete.

Many private schools set their own guidelines and set up their own level of competition and sports achievement. Therefore the onus is on Black parents to perform an in-depth study of private schools they want their athlete to attend. Without such detailed research of the private schools and their athletic programs the athlete may find that going to a private school it is not a bed of roses. Once enrolled it's usually too late and transferring starts the athlete on a roving, gypsy lifestyle of bouncing from school to school to find a basketball home. While mistakes happen and situations change, transferring, especially more than once, is not a pleasant or rewarding experience. Most times the athlete never finds a happy athletic

117

home. Transferring becomes debilitating to academic and social development. It defeats loyalty and continuity. The constant change promotes instability, finger-pointing and excuse making and stunts the acceptance of personal responsibility and the sense of completing tasks. It allows for the athlete to blame his fate on somebody else. It is a troubling existence for a young teenage athlete coming to grips with his athletic vulnerability. Transferring becomes a serious consequence when homework by parents during the selection process is incomplete.

CHAPTER NINE:
AAU Basketball

Amateur Athletic Union (AAU) basketball is the modern day double-edged sword of athletic achievement in the Black community. For many Black athletes, AAU basketball has provided them access to college coaches and scholarship opportunities as well as a chance to travel the country. Still, there is a strong contingent that says AAU basketball fosters hypocrisy, mixed signals, negative emotions, an inflated self-worth, and a belief that basketball is the salvation and solution to all our problems. They conclude that AAU basketball is a good idea gone wrong. One thing is for sure, today's AAU promotes basketball to an excessive level and the message to the athletes is that basketball is number one and everything else is secondary. For Black athletes, AAU is another layer that tells them that chasing basketball and a professional dream is okay and is endorsed by adults.

While officiating AAU basketball years ago, I thought the program had promise. It seemed to be a way for young athletes to get exposure to college coaches. Traveling to national sites, it seemed like a good idea for deprived youngsters who had never left the city or been on an airplane, to be exposed to other venues in life that they might not see otherwise. I can remember the discussion with a Black athlete from Coolidge High School. The young man, upon accepting a scholarship to a rural junior college in Iowa, was confused and startled when he saw a cow. At 20 years old, he had never seen the animal before in his life. Today, AAU is so sophisticated that it accords athletes a chance to visit and see other parts of the country and be exposed to other lifestyles and environments. For Black athletes relegated to their school, playground, mall, and neighborhood, the exposure provided by AAU teams can often be mind-altering and life-changing. Clearly, this is still a positive of AAU, the exposure it can provide for athletes to expand their horizons and for others still, a chance to get a college scholarship.

The legendary career of now NBA Houston Rockets star, Stevie Francis, had its launching pad through AAU basketball. In the late spring of 1996, Francis played in an AAU tournament at Largo High School in Prince George's County with friend Clay Dade, filming the games to send potential schools. He soared onto the scene as a special player who was a late bloomer. At that time of spring, many of the decisions about where athletes would attend college in the fall had been made. Francis did not have a scholarship offer and the outlook was not bright. However, mainly through his play in the AAU tournaments, Francis received a scholarship to San Jacinto Junior College in Texas, eventually becoming an All-American at the University of Maryland, the number two pick in the 1999 NBA draft, and NBA Co-Rookie of the Year. But for every Francis success story there are at least two hundred kids that are shuffled like a deck of cards. They are misled, coerced, pampered, paid, sold, used, and even encouraged to commit misdemeanor crimes.

The initial premise of AAU basketball and its twin, Youth Basketball of America (YBOA), was to provide opportunities for athletes to enhance their skills, give them an activity to stay off the streets, and perhaps be recognized by a college. With recreation budget cutbacks there was a natural void for the AAU and YBOA to fill. But now a whole different dynamic is at work. Part of the AAU has become a "front" for sneaker companies to put together elite all-star teams and showcase them nationally. Interestingly, these showcase events are for the best and most talented players that have already decided on a college or younger, equally talented players, enabling them to easily accept a college scholarship when their time arrives. Many AAU programs today foster a hidden agenda of backroom handshakes and illegal financial inducements, and peddle athletes off to junior colleges for "chump change."

The pursuit of money and the chance to latch onto a rising star has forced a lot of people in positions of leadership with AAU programs to compromise their value system. Meanwhile, the athletes are left with mixed messages, false praise of their athletic-worth and egos far greater than their skill level. In fairness all AAU basketball is not in this category. The multitude of programs in AAU have positive rewards, promote healthy competition and provide opportunities for colleges to view athletes. Unfortunately, it's the excesses of the big time AAU programs that garner sports headlines and bring down the entire program.

The first question that must be asked is how AAU came to wield such tremendous power over athletes? In the middle '80s, AAU was not the pawnbroker and summer juggernaut it is today. AAU was merely a collection of teams assembled to showcase the best athletes from one region against another. A loosely organized collection of all-city, all-county and all-state players was formed to compete against other similarly constructed teams both locally and nationally. It was about competition and geographical bragging rights. AAU basketball was a spring and summer extension of the end of the high school season and included all-star games such as the Dapper Dan in Pittsburgh or the Capital Classic in Washington DC. There was not tremendous pressure to play and many athletes used it as a venue to stay in shape and go head-to-head against talented athletes.

Meanwhile, two ominous, dark clouds were rapidly moving over to rain on the AAU parade. First, the "sneaker wars" were heating up as Adidas, Nike, and, later, Reebok went to outfit the basketball athletes with their shoes. At the ready, and with deep pockets of cash, the sneaker companies sent out the AAU infantry to recruit the best athletes and outfit them in shoes, uniforms, warm-ups, travel bags, and promises of glamorous nationwide trips. Big money was now on the court. There is no greater combustible mixture in the Black community than basketball and big money. It is every kid's dream and every man's foremost solution. AAU basketball would never be the same.

Simultaneous reforms in college basketball recruiting were occurring. Although stories of the excesses and exploitation of college basketball recruiting were commonplace in the sports pages for years and years, the situation nevertheless was not getting better. In fact, with the NCAA tournament evolving into March Madness and bursting into billion dollar TV contracts the pressure to get a piece of the pie forced more outlandish recruiting scandals. The NCAA needed help policing the sport. The NCAA basketball coaches would not step forward to monitor themselves. They knew every detail. They knew what schools were paying players, and how much they were paid. Yet, with a honor among thieves mentality, the coaching fraternity remained silent. With nowhere to turn, the NCAA set rules. Restrictions were made on the number of contacts coaches and schools could make with recruits including home visits and campus visits. Athletes could only be contacted or recruited during certain times of the year and they could not be recruited until a certain age. Athletes could not sign a letter of intent until after their junior year of high school. These changes and others made it difficult for coaches to get the athletes they needed, preferred, and desired to win the NCAA tournament jackpot.

Enter AAU basketball. The coaches fearing that they would lose control of potential recruits quickly made allies of the AAU coaches. Without any restrictions and beyond the jurisdiction of the NCAA, AAU coaches had free access to the players anytime, anywhere, and at any age. In one respect, AAU personnel became the eyes and ears of college coaches. The only foreseeable problem was how to keep AAU coaches financially satisfied to compete against other colleges and do a creditable job of monitoring the athletes.

Once again the sneaker companies came to the rescue. Many college coaches had shoe contracts with their schools so in order for the schools to stay atop the basketball scene, which affords the shoe companies maximum television and national exposure for their products, they both understood what was needed to keep the pipeline filled with the best recruits. Consequently, the decision was made that shoe companies would financially support the more successful AAU programs and teams. An alliance was formed as the sneaker companies partnered with the AAU programs to compete for the attention of athletes, predominately the Black athlete from the big city.

Consequently, if AAU basketball is dirty then there should be quite a few people in the washroom reaching for the soap dispenser. AAU basketball did not become an out of control summer monster overnight. And those that claim that it has too much influence on the athletes have probably been unsuccessful in making an inroad to a successful AAU program and have lost recruits because of this failure. Conversely, those that refuse to look at the embarrassing AAU headlines and to accept blame should have expected abuses within the system. It is impossible to introduce a combination of money and basketball, two of the Black community's most adored passions, and believe that excesses will not happen. This is especially the case when there are minimal restrictions and guidelines for recruiting by AAU programs and coaches.

As a result, today's AAU basketball has levels of participation similar to the NCAA which classifies it universities and colleges into Division I, II, or III. AAU basketball is not played on a level playing field and, like the NCAA divisions, there is a have and have not system predicated on money and clout. With the big money support of the sneaker companies and the alliances formed with certain colleges, many AAU programs can simply overpower smaller and grass root organizations. It is these powerful, well connected, well organized, and well-financed programs that generally make the negative headlines and give all AAU programs a black eye. A distinction must be made regarding big time AAU programs and grassroots organizations.

MYTH NO. 1: The welfare of the athletes at the big time AAU programs is top priority. First and foremost, these elite programs are about getting paid. Today's AAU program is clearly about getting paid through assembling teams of elite athletes and for receiving money off of a talented athlete once he turns professional. Their mission is to procure the best players for the different age brackets within their programs. Hopefully, the most talented players will become "representatives" for a particular shoe company, attend college where that school is equipped by the same shoe company, win a ton of games for the coach, make the Final Four and plenty of national TV games, turn pro and sign a mega-million-dollar deal to represent the shoe company. Everybody is happy; the shoe company gets a recognized pitchman for their shoes, the athlete is rich beyond belief and the college coach and university win games and reap a huge financial bonanza. The AAU coach gets paid by the athlete for his loyalty and "fatherly" guidance and he and his program receive increased financial support and benefits from the shoe companies. With the reputation of having a winning AAU program and former players who now play in the NBA, the pipeline of talented athletes is well-stocked.

The big time AAU programs are persistent. They understand the streets and what is important to youths. They know how far a $20.00 handshake or a new CD can go toward gaining the confidence of a young Black athlete. But mostly their weapons of choice are shoes, athletic gear and apparel, and weekend trips. The AAU reputation is solidified within the sub-culture of high school basketball and athletes value their AAU programs just as much as their school team. AAU programs target athletes and recruit tirelessly all year long. If necessary they "steal" players from other programs and they brazenly recruit while athletes are in school and in preparation for their upcoming seasons.

I remember an unusual incident after officiating a game at Oxon Hill High School during the winter of 1999. As we left the gym about 30 minutes after the game, a collection of five AAU coaches was hovering in the lobby. They were all hoping to speak with the 6'8" 270 lb. Junior, standout center, Michael Sweetney. The star athlete had verbally committed to Georgetown University.

He would be a tremendous catch for any AAU program, but Sweetney was different, he could not be bought or swayed by summer tournaments in Las Vegas or boxes of shoes. He had a sound, stable family. He valued his relationship with his teammates and was loyal to his coach. They could not influence Sweetney. He did play AAU, but with a small area team comprised of friends. In March of 2000, Oxon Hill won the Maryland State 4A championship and Sweetney was named the Washington DC male Athlete of the Year.

MYTH NO. 2: The big time AAU programs will get college scholarship offers for athletes in their programs. Sure, athletes that have played with various AAU programs get scholarships, but that does not necessarily mean it was as a result of the AAU. Most big time AAU athletes are the elite from a given area. They are very familiar to college recruiters and barring academic concerns would receive a scholarship regardless of the AAU.

MYTH NO. 3: AAU programs will expose Black athletes to new and different places. Most athletes have scholarships to Division I programs and will play colleges nationwide. However, many athletes are indeed exposed to different things. A junior high school coach in Washington DC tells of how one of his former athletes attended a big time AAU program spent his 18th birthday while on the road at a tournament. Apparently, his AAU coach solicited the services of a prostitute to the athlete's hotel room to celebrate his birthday.

The smaller grass roots AAU teams are throwbacks to what AAU was intended. The leaders of these programs are men and women with a genuine concern for young people. Many get involved because they have sons and daughters who want to compete, but are turned off by the intensity and tactics of big time programs. Others get involved under the misconception that AAU is the way for their child to earn an athletic scholarship. Whatever the reasons, many of the coaches and program coordinators for these teams are likeable, sincere, and committed. Their programs are a collection of local youth from a given community or school district and the majority of their success comes from smaller AAU tournaments. The athletes play hard but the teams just don't have the resources, manpower, or energy and inclination to procure the elite talent required to compete on the national level. This is the category that most AAU programs fall under.

It is interesting to speak with directors of smaller AAU teams. After going head to head in competition against the big time programs and fending them off from taking their better players, many admit that they underestimated the subculture of high school basketball. Many say the experience is physically taxing and mentally draining. For others, it fortifies their resolve to promote a proper example for athletes. These smaller programs value effort, teamwork, and character.

MYTH NO. 4: AAU is the best way to get an athletic scholarship. AAU participation in the big city is almost exclusively by Black athletes. Many falsely assume that a scholarship is always available. A scholarship will be forthcoming only if a player has talent, pure and simple. If a player can play and has academics to supplement his athletic skills, the colleges will find him or her. It will not matter whether they are at a public or private school, whether they play AAU or summer league, or go to summer camps. The recruiting by colleges for qualified student athletes is intense and all encompassing. Each year more colleges move into Division I basketball (at the conclusion of the 2000-2001 season the total was 319 up from 294 in 1997.) In order to compete at that level, they must have talented student athletes.

AAU can afford an athlete more chances to play against good competition and possibly catch the eye of a college scout. But it is no more of a chance than for an athlete who remains academically eligible to compete on his high school team. The bottom line is that there is no substitute for athletic talent and usually the cream will rise to the top.

At the 1999 Charlie Webber Invitational basketball tournament, a novel grass roots concept was created. Four Prince George's County public high school basketball coaches formed an alliance and placed in the tournament many of the top high school players from around the county. The four coaches, Billy Lanier from Oxon Hill High, Walter Fulton from Central High, Glenn Farello from Eleanor Roosevelt High and Steve Matthews from Gwynn Park High were fed up with the underhanded and overbearing tactics administered by larger AAU programs.

It was an attempt to take control away from the AAU coaches and return it to the schools. The coaches acknowledged the importance of showcasing the athletes in the AAU national tournament attended by over 250 college coaches, but they did not accept the premise that it had to be done solely through an AAU program. The idea was an unselfish act by the coaches. They could just as easily have been golfing or fishing. These four coaches came together and knew the criticism they would receive. The results were fantastic. Prince George's County athletes represented themselves capably against some of the big time AAU programs of the country. Furthermore, they disproved the previously held notion that only major AAU programs can garner exposure for athletes.

Probably the most obscure, overlooked, and stepped on member of the high school subculture is the public school coach. These men and women have the thankless job of trying to field a competitive team each year. Each season seems harder than the last as the recruitment by private schools, AAU programs, and colleges gets more intense. Everybody knows that public schools cannot compete with the glamourous trappings and bright lights offered by private schools and AAU programs. Heck, many public schools, especially in the Black community, can't ensure the bare essentials of a safe environment and a quality education. Yet there the public high school coach remains optimistic about the upcoming season, always anxious to get started and always trying to prepare young men and women for their first step on the new horizon. The $2500-$3500 stipend they receive for coaching is probably less than minimum wage when factored into the actual time spent on behalf of the athletes. The public school coach like the public school teacher must wear a multitude of different hats to communicate and reach today's troubled youth. Their work is truly a labor of love for youth and the game of basketball.

Big time AAU basketball is not about balance. It is strictly basketball and then more basketball. Some say that is all it should be about and that balance should be provided by parents and teachers. This is fine but AAU, with its focus on winning basketball games, recruiting, and money, sends the wrong message to Black youth already confused about their value system and identity.

While AAU should not be sought for balance, neither should it hasten the Black athletes' dependence on hoops for their salvation. AAU basketball with all its grandiose trappings and shady, underhanded shenanigans illustrates that ethics and morals are on the bench and that winning basketball games is the only hustle. This only amplifies the Black athletes' addiction to hoops and elevates the false perception that basketball *is* the solution instead of basketball leading to a solution. Mixed signals abound and the athletes watch and listen and unconsciously place an exaggerated value on basketball and what it can do for them. As young men and women it is hard for them to do anything else.

I had several conversations with an outstanding guard-forward from a nationally ranked private school who had already signed to play basketball in the ACC. The young man played AAU basketball with a team in Atlanta. He was flown from the Washington DC area to Atlanta, courtesy of his AAU team, to compete in tournaments. The athlete is a nice, bright young man with aspirations of playing professionally. But when you are personally flown in and out of town like a corporate CEO delivering the annual report to stockholders, how can a teenager keep an even keel relationship with basketball?

Mixed message to young athletes: *My game is sweet as apple pie. Everybody wants me and I'm on the path to NBA stardom. My dream is near, I just have to keep playing basketball. I don't need to become a well-rounded person. I don't need to develop positive relationships with my peers and especially women. I don't need to subject myself to authority including my parents, teachers and coaches. And I definitely don't need school or to study. I got game; everybody knows it and I'm headed for the League.*

In the summer of 1999, two leaders of strong winning AAU programs in the Washington area, Jeff Brooks, the program leader and coach of the Jabbo Kenner AAU teams and Rob Johnson, the director and sometime coach of the Silver Spring Blue Devils AAU programs, got into a heated shouting match over an athlete at the conclusion of an AAU game. Both men vehemently argued that the player should be playing with their respective team and accused the other of stealing. With the athletes watching, the men had to be separated by assistant coaches. Grown Black men in leadership roles almost came to blows over recruitment of an athlete.

Mixed message to young athletes: *Basketball is serious business. They really need me to be successful. They will give me anything I want because I'm the best player since Kobe. I am somebody because I can dunk a basketball.*

Alternate message: *If we can't agree then let's "throw down" and do battle. Physical violence is an acceptable alternative through which to resolve our differences.*

In the spring of 2000, Potomac Valley AAU chairman Norman Smith told me that the problem of coaches urging older players to use doctored and phony birth certificates (a misdemeanor crime in Maryland) so they can play in a younger age bracket was so rampant that AAU National headquarters threatened expulsion of the teams, coaches, and players.

Mixed message to young athlete: *The hustle is okay. Forget about authority and rules. Do what you got to do to get over. We need to win at all cost, baby.*

A complaint I have heard numerous times from the smaller AAU programs is the blatant and arrogant ways big time programs attempt to raid and steal players from them. It seems to get worse every year, but the same methods are employed every time. An AAU coach approaches an athlete with the sales pitch of, "If you join our team we will give you free sneakers, apparel, and gym bags. We have great new uniforms. We will pay all your dues and membership fees. We will travel to other cities, stay in nice hotels and play in more tournaments than your current team. The college recruiters will see you. And we will win." What is striking about this conversation is the fact that it takes place at a game site, possibly even after the teams have just competed against each other.

Mixed message to young athlete: *They want to give me all this and all I have to do is play ball. This is great. It isn't hard work. It's stealing, man. And it will only get better when I get to the NBA and really get paid. Loyalty, commitment, and responsibility to others? That's for those that don't have options. I'm in demand. I don't have time to wait.*

Many grass roots and small organizations that qualify to compete in the national AAU tournaments in cities such as Orlando, or Memphis, or Seattle, but are without a sponsor and need money for plane fares and hotel accommodations. They have to fundraise and become resourceful in order to get the thousands of dollars needed for the trip. One less than creative measure that coaches use to raise money is to send the players (usually the younger groups of 10-14 year olds) out on heavily-traveled intersections wearing their jerseys with buckets and signs to beg for loose change from cars. Despite the flawed concept it is also the one with the fastest reward. Coaches and parents tell me that on the "right corner on the right day" (usually on government pay weeks) teams can collect up to $1000 or more for a 4 to 5 hour stay on Friday evening or Saturday afternoon. It is still a poorly thought out and shortsighted idea.

First of all, it is not the safest approach to have kids darting between stopped vehicles. Secondly, it is a busy and crowded corner to share in the big city. There is the Nation of Islam representative selling the latest edition of the *Final Call* and bean pies. The windshield wiper crew is on hand to clean your windows for change. There is the panhandler with the requisite, "Homeless. Please help. Thank you. God Bless" sign. And don't forget the young hustlers hawking CD's, incense, and other ill-gotten booty possibly pilfered from the strip mall across the street.

Lastly, and most importantly, these are the same coaches that told the athletes in AAU games just a couple of days ago to play hard, never quit, and keep fighting. These are the same coaches that preached to referees that their teams have worked too hard to have their game taken away by bad calls. Now, instead of working to acquire the necessary funds through a car wash or bake sale the coach sends Black youth to the hazardous streets to beg with a sign and a smile. The last thing Black youth need to be taught is to rely on charity from others. Self-respect is attained only through hard work and accomplishment.

Mixed message to young athletes: *It's okay to beg. People will give Black people something for nothing, just like welfare. Black folks don't have to work hard anywhere else but on the* *basketball court. With a good hustle there is always a way to get something for nothing.*

There is no reasonable way to expect teenagers to put their AAU recruitment and overall experience in a proper perspective. This is especially true of young Black athletes who believe their only redeeming value, their only way above the apathy of their existence and only escape from their environment is through their ability to play basketball. They watch as adults fight, lie, steal, and break rules to get athletes. They see the promises and the money that is used to entice athletes to play in their programs. Black athletes are already aware of the star status accorded basketball players and AAU becomes another reason to do nothing else but play ball. It does not require a twisting of the arm of Black youth to get them to play basketball. The Black athlete, already in hot pursuit of a pro career, is just learning how to take advantage of his skills and get paid even before turning professional. Balance is lost. Basketball is king. AAU paves the road of becoming hooked on hoops.

Every year several athletes finish the season with one public high school, join an AAU roster with obvious ties to another school and the following season are enrolled at the preferred school of the AAU program. The impetus for the change the influence of his AAU coach who was able to convince the athlete through an out of state tournament, sneakers, and a warm-up suit that transferring was in the best interest of the athlete. Loyalty is not an issue. However, this can engender an athlete that is unapproachable, hard to coach, and devoid of an honest assessment of his abilities.

Too much attention and praise heaped on young athletes who are passionate about hoops and are under tremendous pressure to perform will eventually generate severe problems. Like a heavy, steady rain after the ground is saturated, where excess water will find a way to run off through streams and puddles, so too will the too early recruitment of Black athletes, unaccustomed to the spotlight, cause other problems with inflated egos and a codependent relationship with basketball. The attention and acclaim from recruiters, adults, parents, the media, and the high social standings within the Black community are overpowering and captivating. A young teenage Black athlete can't help but get swept up in the fanfare and glory. He misunderstands that the fame and adulation is for what he is instead of who he is. But who he is and what he is about is a whole different dynamic that gets lost in the frenzy of athletic stardom. Young Black athletes that never established a true identity before acheiving basketball success readily accept their hoop fame. It contrasts their hard scrabble, invisible upbringing and they are all to willing to accept what they have become instead of searching for who they are. And now, any self-evaluation is predicated on winning basketball games and athletic achievement. Big time AAU programs often promote this concept with their "basketball is first mentality."

CHAPTER TEN:
Nomadic Basketball Stars

The next major rule change in college basketball will not involve the exodus of underclassmen to the NBA, but instead will center on the transferring of athletes to other schools. If you listen to college coaches, announcers, and commentators the egos of athletes are a major source of frustration and consternation. Athletes transfer colleges with starting positions guaranteed for the upcoming season. They give a multitude of self-serving, me-first reasons for their action such as, "The coach's style was not best suited to my game," or "I can play my natural position at another school," or perhaps, "I need to play the position I will play in the NBA." Ironically, this "look out for number one, I'm the greatest" attitude of the athletes was started by the coaches, recruiters, and AAU leaders.

To expect the same athlete to understand his role and exhibit virtues such as patience, trust, obligation, and respect just because he is in college is naive. College, to the athlete, is just the next, brief, and last step on his ladder to the NBA. Therefore, at the first hint of basketball trouble, frustration, or disciplinary issues with the coach the athlete says, "I don't need this," and looks elsewhere.

An assistant coach at a Big East school told me that all the athletes they recruit think they are already prepared for the pros. In fact, the coach called this problem the "Allen Iverson Syndrome", where Black athletes strive to be like the Philadelphia 76ers All-star guard. Apparently, Black athletes identify with the fact that Iverson went to jail, then went to a prominent school like Georgetown, did not graduate and is now in the pros making "big bank" his way. They see his small frame and assume that they are just as good, but bigger and will make the grade. They fail to see Iverson's heart, passion, and desire, which are second to none.

Transferring will always be a part of high school and college basketball. For athletes to pick the "right" school and for recruiters to select the "right" player is, at best, a subjective art. Mistakes will be made. Every season athletes sign with college programs that are clearly above their basketball skill level. The athlete shouldn't be faulted when the bigger schools come calling. It is an ego boost to have a big time program show interest in your skills. Mixed signals abound and it takes a rare athlete to evaluate his talents honestly and place himself in the right situation. The athlete needs the support and encouragement of parents and a good high school coach, because he cannot make a sound decision regarding his athletic prospects in college. He believes that he is the best and he can play at the highest level. He reasons that the schools would not have offered him a scholarship if he did not have the ability to play at the school. I have watched over the last 25 years as a couple hundred athletes in the Washington DC area alone have signed with college programs, never played and eventually transferred. The scenario is the same each year.

The athlete's name starts to hit the recruiting circles. He plays well at the cattle auctions atmosphere of summer camps and AAU tournaments. He has a successful season and plays particularly well the night the recruiter from Big Time University is in the stands. Press clippings and post-season accolades follow. Big Time U. steps up the recruiting process. However, what is often not being told to Mr. All-Local talent is that Big Time U. is also looking at three other players from around the country for the same wing guard position. Mr. All-Local Talent is the third choice and Big Time U. is hedging its bet in case the other players commit elsewhere or fail to pass the SAT exam. Meanwhile, Mr. All-Local Talent is on Cloud Nine. He watches Big Time U. on ESPN. The school has a nice run through March Madness, winning a game or two. He listens as announcers recite that the starting wing guard is graduating. Equally as important, his teammates, friends, and relatives hear that Big Time U. is interested in him inflating his ego and elevating his status in the basketball subculture.

Nomadic Basketball Stars

Out the window is the fact that all other inquiries about Mr. All-Local Talent were from smaller colleges or perhaps from Division II. But he isn't concerned with the premise that maybe that is his true talent level. He has convinced himself that Big Time U. knows what he has known all along—that he can play the game. So, while friends, teammates, and family boast, he loses his perspective and he is devoid of a voice of reason. Even the high school coach can lose his perspective. Some coaches, especially at private schools, understand the recruiting tool available to them. The coach can go into the homes of eighth and ninth graders and sell the fact that he has sent Mr. All-Local Talent to Big-Time U. Meanwhile, with the blessings of his support system, Mr. All-Local Talent accepts the scholarship offer from Big Time U.

It immediately becomes a frustrating experience academically, socially, and athletically. He is competing against mature young men. After all, he is an 18 year old playing against juniors and seniors who are 21 years of age. The experience can be daunting, and the athlete heads home and transfers. Sometimes lost in the abundance of games on television is the fact that athletes that play basketball at the Division I level are very talented, skilled, and large young men. Until you have been on the floor with these athletes or watched the game up close and in person you take for granted just how physically and intellectually gifted they are and the instincts they bring to the court. There is no greater college athlete than a basketball player. High school athletes that receive accolades and respect fail to understand the tremendous leap in the caliber of play and skill level.

Athletes today are oblivious to this fact. They sincerely believe that their skill level is exceptional and that they will start immediately on the college level. The player believes the hype, about his rock solid game and fails to consider that there is always someone bigger and better. At the Division I level, every athlete, including bench personnel, was probably first team All-Something from their respective areas. In fact, many high school stars including scoring champions end up at lower Division I programs. These players are talented, but the major differences as athletes move from high school to college are physical size, strength, and fundamentally sound basketball skills. Playing basketball in college is not a given regardless of what peers, teammates, or newspapers recommend. Moving up to college should not be taken as mere formality but many Black athletes see it as an athletic rite of passage. It is shallow thinking and clearly a mistake.

Basketball skill can be enhanced and improved upon with hard, diligent effort. If the athlete has the quickness and a desire to he can improve his skills. Athletes often have a late growth spurt, but in most cases, size does not change. In particular, positional size is probably the most underestimated factor by athletes moving from high school to college and college to professional. Usually as athletes go from high school to Division I college and from college to pro, their position goes down. For example, centers in high school become power forwards in college, or even point guards in the pros. The best illustration is NBA great Hersey Hawkins. He was a 6'3" center in high school in Chicago. He went to Bradley University in Illinois and led the nation in scoring as a forward. Later in the pros, measuring 6'5", Hawkins played exclusively as a long range shooting guard his entire career. He played over 10 years and made millions of dollars but he had to downsize his position from center to forward to guard. Hawkins worked hard to expand his skills to compensate for size. Black athletes who seek to reach the next level must understand the importance of improving their skills in order to play basketball well. Unfortunately, many athletes arrogantly assume that their game is good and underestimate the college level competition. The skill level of many athletes never improves. Naturally, their careers levels off and the athletes are at a loss to explain why.

There are two primary reasons for this situation. First, many athletes simply play basketball games and seldom have supervised practice. Basketball leagues and tournaments are year round. As a result, the athlete plays all year, but does not work on his game. Game competition does not substitute for individual work to improve and expand basketball skills. In game situations, athletes are not going to work on a weakness. They will instinctively and competitively do what they do best. Thus, a 6'4", 215 lb. high school power forward needing a perimeter jump shot for the college level will only shoot lay-ins and dunks in competitive game situations. A 5'11" shooting guard who needs to become a point guard and learn how to distribute the ball, set up teammates for baskets and run an offense refuses to handle the ball except to launch three pointers.

Comfort and pride will not allow the athletes to alter their game, work on a weakness, and risk potential embarrassment during game situations. Thus their games level off and the inevitable crash is near. They don't understand that playing games does not improve your skills. Games must be supplemented with individual and fundamental work and development. Playing against better competition can make an athlete tougher, more resourceful, and more imaginative, but without individual practice and hard work, the skill level does not improve.

The second area where athletes fall short in their relationship with basketball is misinterpreting love for the game as passion for the game. In interviews with high school coaches the one common theme, repeated time after time is the lack of a work ethic by players. The coaches collectively say, "The kids today don't want to work at the game. The kids love the game, they love to play, but they do not have a passion for the game." Passion for basketball is an inner desire or fire that consumes a player to the point where he constantly hungers to expand his knowledge, skill level, and dedication to the game. A passionate player is always searching for new ways to improve.

According to many high school coaches, most young athletes today lack the passion to really excel at the game of basketball. They want the fancy material trappings of big NBA money, huge houses, and multiple cars, yet athletes fail to see the hard work, dedication, and practice that are required to reach the top of the NBA. The young athlete seems oblivious when the superstar athletes of the NBA speak of the endless hours of solitude spent shooting 500 or more jump shots, the grueling long distance running regimes, or the exhausting and painful weight training programs. The young athlete even ignores the professional athletes' concept of proper rest and diet.

Coaches blame to society for the athlete's *lack* of passion. They point to "how it is very easy to be lazy"—drive through windows for food, microwave ovens for meals, Internet, cell phones, and Playstation games for fast access to information and entertainment, and cable TV with over 200 channels. It is easy to become distracted and while athletes continue to play organized basketball year round, they mistakenly assume they are improving just by playing the game.

CHAPTER ELEVEN:
The Myth of Early Entry into the NBA Draft

During the summer of 1999, I was officiating a high school summer league all-star game on the campus of Georgetown University. A young, talented athlete soared to the hoop and was fouled as he laid the ball in the basket. Just before I awarded the player the basketball for his subsequent free throw shot, I complimented him on a great move. The young Black athlete glanced toward me, smiled and said, "Thanks, Mr. Ref, I'm gonna be the next Kobe."

His statement weighed a ton. I instantly felt old; "Be Like Mike" had suddenly become passé. Young Black athletes not only want to be like Lakers super star Kobe Bryant because of his great skill and larger than life persona, they gravitate to the idea of jumping straight to the professional ranks from high school just like he did. After all, this is something that even the greatest, Michael Jordan, did not do. Make no mistake about it—high school athletes want the NBA dream. And, if possible, most prefer the dream by the fast track traveled by Kobe Bryant.

The trend of high school athletes opting for the NBA is probably here to stay. And each year, according to the experts, expect the list of names of high school and college players declaring early entry into the NBA draft to increase. Many within sports including NBA commissioner David Stern publicly say it has become a cultural issue especially in the Black community. This, however, is an inaccurate, unsubstantiated, forecast of impending doom rooted in politics and hidden agendas that once again uses the Black male and Black community as the pawns of choice. In the '50s, '60s and early '70s, it was accepted within the sports culture that if you wanted to play in the NBA your journey had to include four years of college basketball. Athletes played the game with the same passion and commitment as the players of today, perhaps even more so, but they had no quick fix or shortcut to the NBA. Four years of college was the only road to the NBA.

In 1970, Spencer Haywood, an All-American forward for the University of Detroit, sued the NBA to allow him to enter the league prior to completing his college eligibility. Haywood left college early and was playing in the American Basketball Association (ABA) at the time. Prior to the legal test case involving Haywood, the NBA prohibited the drafting or signing of a player before his college class had graduated. Haywood argued that as the sole wage earner for his family he was a "hardship case" and had a right to begin earning a living. The Supreme Court ruled in Haywood's favor and in 1971, the NBA adopted the "hardship rule." In 1976, the "hardship rule" was eliminated in favor of the current Early Entry standard now in place.

In essence this decision started the trend that today has filtered down to high school athletes who view attending college as nothing more than a distraction or annoyance. They see the NBA scouts at their high school games and they have watched the success of other high school athletes. Kobe Bryant, Kevin Garnett, and Tracy McGrady have become NBA all-stars, multi-millionaires, and pop culture icons. Today, the popular theory among young adults is, " why hang around college for four years? Get the money and run. A college degree? What for? Get it later in the off-season!"

Is early entry for college athletes or skipping college altogether an isolated occurrence relegated to just a few super-talented Black youngsters? Or is it the seed of a pervasive cultural attitude that once again seeps into our sports community like drugs and the lottery?

Roughly 25-35 high school and college basketball players have claimed early entry status each year over the last several years. In 2001, a huge increase occurred as 58 underclassmen and high school players initially declared early entry into the NBA draft. Everyone involved with sports on all levels sounded the alarm of concern over the misguided athletes, the decay of our country's moral and value systems, and the corresponding devaluation of education. I fail to see it this way considering that the athletes that leave college early represent less than one percent of all NCAA Division I and II Basketball players. (The percentage does not include the thousands of athletes that compete in Division III, National Association of Intercollegiate Athletics (NAIA) and National Junior College Athletic Association (NJCAA). But of course these athletes are not on television nightly.)

So, why are we so obsessed with the 40 to 50 athletes or less than one percent that leave school early for the NBA draft? One primary reason is the outcry from the glamorous, high profile, power schools in Division I college basketball. They do not want to lose these players every year, because it detracts from their ability to stay atop the college basketball world. However, shed no tears for these institutions. They will still reap their millions of dollars, appear a dozen times or more on national television, and participate in the NCAA tournament. Their hollow and insincere cry has nothing to do with the welfare of the athletes but rather reflects their concern over having to reload their systems and possibly sacrifice wins while orienting a new crop of blue chip athletes.

Another cluster of colleges are considered middle majors. They are categorized as mid-major universities for many reasons, but mainly for the fact that they play in the shadow of the power teams and usually recruit players that the bigger schools overlooked. Consequently, they rarely have players that are skilled enough to declare early entry to the NBA and they usually keep their players for four years. Privately, the middle majors see the early exit of players from the rosters of the big schools as an opportunity for an upset, especially in the NCAA tournament where wins can provide exposure, expanded recruiting opportunities, and increase revenue for their universities. Schools such as Gonzaga and Kent State have had such success. Therefore, the mid-majors do not shed buckets of tears for the early entry athletes moving on. Clearly, it is the power schools, along with their running mate, television, that fan the flames of dismay over early entry.

There is a school of thought about the Black community that the trend towards athletes leaving college early or never enrolling is now a socially accepted and expected part of Black basketball. In fact, sports hierachy say it is a "test of manhood" or rite of passage. Apparently, according to the "experts", the Black athlete now has a complete disregard for playing four years of college and subsequently getting his degree. In fact, they imply that the Black sports culture considers the athlete that plays four years in college as weak, a sellout for the educational system who lacks a true, big time game. Some felt that way about Shane Battier, a four year starter for 2001 national champion Duke University.

This is simply not true. First, more athletes return for their sophomore, junior, and senior year in college than apply for early NBA entry. It is the extremely gifted athletes who leave early and this differentiation must be made clear. Furthermore, at the high school level most athletes are ecstatic just to get a Division I scholarship much less leap into the NBA. The desire to go pro is real for high school athletes, but the reality and options are not. Washington DC, acknowledged as one of the top areas for high school basketball in our country has less than two dozen basketball athletes each year that receive scholarships to the Division I basketball power conferences like the ACC, Big Ten and Big East. The NBA is still a lottery-ticket dream for most Black athletes and will always remain so.

Second, do not fault the Black community for the growing number of early entries to the NBA draft. This is a typical theme: Blame Black society for America's ills. Young athletes leaving early for the NBA is symptomatic of youth everywhere. Where was the media's outrage over White youth going pro in tennis, golf, and baseball? Could this be racial envy? The NBA publicly says the right things about its concern for players, but its actions say something different. It has been over 30 years since Spencer Haywood and the Hardship clause and the problem over players leaving school early did not happen overnight.

Thirty years ago, Black athletes accepted that four years of college was the only way to reach the NBA. However, after four years many athletes did not graduate and were simply shuffled through fluff courses to maintain their eligibility. Now, extremely gifted athletes do not have to wait in the NBA's "minor league"— also known as the NCAA. In fact, more athletes should test early entry, but without signing with an agent in order to preserve the option of returning to school. It makes good marketing sense and provides a valuable learning experience as well as a better understanding of NBA requirements.

The Black community is not as naïve as the NBA and NCAA might think. In fact, it is insulting to suggest that early NBA entry is a "test of manhood" comparable to a gang initiation ritual. The Black athlete is only playing the game of early entry within the rules that the NBA and NCAA designed. In the '60s when four years of college was required before going into the NBA, the Black athlete complied. Now, decades later, the Black athlete continues to play within the boundaries. But because early entry provides the Black athlete with options, while alternately causing frustration and inconvenience for the NBA, NCAA and their coaches, the perceived problem is the deviant, and supposedly academically uncommitted Black community.

The "test of manhood" statement made by NBA Commissioner Stern and some college coaches is grossly irresponsible, erroneous, and borderline racist. How can these "experts" proclaim an educational crisis within the Black community based on the NBA dreams of less than 50 athletes a year? How can a handful of extremely gifted athletes override the diligence, perseverance, and aspirations of the other 5000 athletes playing college basketball each season, or the over 15,000 plus Black men and women student athletes that compete yearly in Division I collegiate sports? For that matter, how can they discredit and ignore the 1.4 million Black coed undergraduate students enrolled in all colleges nationwide? Let's be perfectly clear—The focus should not be on the athletes leaving early for the NBA, but on the thousands of athletes that play four years of college and still fail to receive a college degree.

The Black community in my opinion is not in opposition to a college education, rather it is aware that the NCAA does not act in the best interest of the athlete. It is cognizant of the fact that colleges exploit our Black youth by feeding them an unbalanced diet of low graduation rates and abysmal employment opportunities while they feast on a $6 billion TV contract. Meanwhile, NBA teams enthusiastically and willingly select our high school athletes and early entry players and pay them millions of dollars. Yes, casualties happen—many athletes will not be drafted and will lose their college eligibility in the process—but casualties also occur when Black athletes are fed through the meat-grinder of college athletics such that three out of every four Division I Black basketball players currently leave school without their degrees. However, at that time the concern of the NCAA or NBA is non-existent because like loyal troops, these athletes have already served the institution's purpose well.

The Black community understands that it is a very rare and extremely gifted athlete that can skip college and move straight to the pros. In addition, that athlete is usually near 7 feet. Kobe Bryant at 6'6" was the shortest athlete to have success. Even Dajuan Wagner, a 6'2" guard from Camden, New Jersey considered by many to be the best high school player in the nation in 2000-2001, opted for college at the University of Memphis rather than try his hand immediately in the NBA. His decision to attend college instead of the NBA was probably correct, but yet extremely difficult. The proper choice was made despite tremendous pressure from media, fans, peers, agents, friends, and community, all of whom were captivated by his fabulous athletic gifts.

Boo Williams, the moderator of a large, well-organized AAU tournament held each April, told WTEM sports talk radio that the

The Myth of Early Entry into the NBA Draft

entourage that followed Wagner, the 2001 *USA TODAY* high school player of the year, was comparable in size to that which probably accompanied Muhammad Ali. In fact, Ali is a good comparison. The addiction to adulation and big money is so captivating that it drove Ali, Sugar Ray Leonard, and Roberto Duran back into the boxing ring way past their prime. If these sports legends and others can't resist the limelight after retiring in their late 30s and 40s, should we expect anything different from our youth?

Many exceptional athletes consult the NBA to assess their draft potential. Unfortunately, many leave college too early because they listened to the wrong people. Regretfully, they are not drafted in the first round which guarantees a salary. They may not ever get drafted in the second round. The worst scenario is leaving college early and never being drafted. Many gifted athletes who were not drafted have limited options. They play with various semi-pro teams, the new National Basketball Developmental League, or overseas. This is a far cry from their hooked on hoops dreams.

CHAPTER TWELVE
Why Black Athletes Fail to Graduate from College

Ask any segment of the Black community why Black athletes fail to graduate from college, and you are headed for an emotional and opinionated discourse. Ask Black athletes that did not get their degrees and you will get one opinion. Ask Black athletes that have their degrees and you will receive yet another rationale. Ask Black men and women that have graduated from college but did not play sports and an altogether different perspective will be forthcoming. Ask parents of the athletes that have been to college or are headed to school and other concerns are raised. Ask the teaching, administrative, and coaching professionals at the high schools that prepare the athletes and the colleges that accept them and still different theories are presented. The only common denominator is the firmness of their responses to the debate, although many were not aware of just how serious an issue it is and were astounded at the abysmal graduation rates.

While a central explanation cannot be pinpointed, perhaps the real reason is the Black community itself. True, it is very easy to cast extensive blame on the colleges for their exploitation of the Black athlete for their financial gain. Hall of Fame coach and mentor of Georgetown University basketball for 27 years, John Thompson, readily acknowledges and has said publicly that universities exploit Black athletes. The issues of racial isolation, prejudice, ignorance, and even unsafe campus surroundings are a concern as athletes from Black urban environments are thrust into a new, culturally different, predominately White and sometimes unfriendly setting. These matters are often treated with only a whisper, if at all, by the college hierarchy. Of course, we can easily find fault with the big business, super intense, survival of the athletically fittest aspects of the college scholarship as Black athletes try to come to grips with the vulnerability of their basketball talents for the first time in their lives. And let's not forget the high stakes, must win, revenue driven college coaches and athletic departments that often provide "lip-service" but little else to the issue of graduation of Black athletes. Winning basketball games and generating income are clearly the first priority of most athletic programs instead of educating Black young men. All have a share in the reason for poor graduation rates among Black athletes.

Yet, these are institutional obstacles, similar to racial profiling by police for example, that will be slow to change but must be brought to light. Certainly, change will never occur if the Black community is content to sneak only a few players to the NBA while most of our athletes fail to capitalize on the opportunity for an education and, instead, fall like leaves from the trees in autumn. The Black community has all the tools to empower Black athletes and we must teach our athletes to exhibit perseverance and tenacity in order to ascend beyond these barriers. Our history, (if we choose to study it—another topic for discussion) speaks to our conquering spirit. We have survived the middle passage, slavery, and day-to-day racism to become valued, sought after, and cherished by a White structure that is willing to provide us a $60,000 or more education at America's highest institutions of learning. For perspective, during slavery not long ago we were beaten, sold or possibly killed for even trying to learn to read. The burden our athletes carry today does not compare to that of our ancestors. Therefore, regardless of the inequitable system in place, we must seize the opportunity and we must graduate.

Unfortunately, what precludes our athletes from graduating is a Black community that is largely consumed with Black athletic success. Consequently, we produce hooked on hoops athletes that are caught in the grasp of sports idolatry far before they get to college where it is often too late to see the value of an education.

As early as junior high school, our Black athletes have been allowed to slide in the classroom as grades are given, papers and tests are written or taken by others, attendance is ignored and education is devalued. Deviant, crass, and obnoxious behavior on and off the court has been excused and rationalized, while adults turn the other cheek or offer the proverbial ninth or tenth "second chance." Hooked on hoops athletes have been deluged with extravagant praise and tribute for their physical gifts. They have been encouraged to think about the "league" now, rather than later. They are cajoled to consider baskets over books, celebrity and money over education, and NBA over college. There has not been a contrary thought or action provided by almost anyone in their immediate circle. Ever since youth league basketball, AAU and high school coaches, national camps, high pressure agents and shoe company reps, college recruiters and NBA scouts, all have bowed to his physical talents. They have glorified his basketball accomplishments, and blotted his self-worth as he takes to the fast lane of a supposedly professional career. Under this type of onslaught, a college education has no value to the Black athlete and his stay on campus will be brief, if it occurs at all.

Almost all high school basketball players that have enjoyed success on the court and acclaim for their talents have experienced this type of hooked on hoops, glorified and privileged status at one point or another. However, the overwhelming majority of high school athletes do not have the supreme basketball talent to consider the immediate option of going to the NBA. Still, the NBA is the goal of high school athletes and college, but not necessarily the college degree, is viewed as a necessary part of the equation. The hooked on hoops athlete takes the NBA dream from high school to college with the belief that he is one step closer to his long time goal. It is a hard truth that almost every basketball athlete on scholarship and starting on his college team thinks that he will play in the NBA. The college diploma is clearly a distant and lackluster second choice.

John Chaney, Hall of Fame basketball coach at Temple University in Philadelphia, spoke with me about this dilemma. Arguably, no coach in college basketball today loves the Black athlete more than John Chaney. He has shown his devotion and commitment to the Black athlete by his actions and deeds throughout his entire coaching career. He immediately attempts to teach his new recruits and players the importance "of the 4 R's: Rules, Roles, Responsibilities, and Respect." Coach Chaney feels that Black athletes miss the big picture of the college education, though it is not entirely the fault of the athlete. Coach Chaney says, "That probably 80 to 90 percent of the kids I have recruited to Temple have one parent or less [at home]." Consequently, most Black athletes "think their primary job is to become a millionaire. They see a future, a window of opportunity from 12 to 22 to make it. But what about the rest of their life? They don't understand to build enough bricks or harvest enough crops to handle age 25 to 80."

Unfortunately, there are not enough coaches like John Chaney at our universities. And while it is the responsibility of the coach as a teaching member of the university to graduate his players, it is the responsibility of the Black community to prepare a well-rounded person and not just an athlete. When the Black community does not adequately prepare our athletes for the college environment, they get lost in the high society glamour and celebration, and the million-dollar pressure-cooker environment of major college athletics. In other words, they remain attached to the hooked on hoops adulation and false security they received as a youth and prep star in their own community. Only now, the consequences and repercussions are at the highest and most severe level.

* High Society Basketball *

The Black athlete's journey from the Black community to big-time college athletics to a possible NBA career is so captivating and intoxicating that he never stops to take a personal inventory of what is transpiring around him. Not until his college eligibility has expired and he is 30 credits or more shy of his degree and the NBA, semi-pro, European, and oversees leagues no longer offer contracts for his basketball talents, does he take an inward look at his whirlwind, roller-coaster- ride, college experience. Then reality sets in, followed in many cases by resentment, bitterness, and a sense of violation, pity, and insecurity. I have had hundreds of conversations with athletes that have played college basketball and clearly, the majority have experienced many of these same emotions once they are removed from the game. For many athletes that played in the high profile, premier conferences like the ACC, Big Ten or Big East, their sports ride was such an exhilarating, energizing, ego-gratifying, grandiose journey that an introspective view of the surroundings was never taken.

In fact, they rejoice in the retelling of their experiences with the big-time aura of college basketball. Former athletes enjoyed their celebrity status and benefits. They speak fondly of their ability to walk into pizza parlors and restaurants and have their tabs picked up simply because of their status on the basketball team. They relished the discounts they received at sporting goods stores or certain clothing stores.

They also enjoyed how their schoolwork assignments, classes, selected professors, and tutors were usually coordinated by academic advisors and athletic department personnel, keeping them free to just play basketball. For many Black athletes from poor environments, they knew for the first time in their lives they would have three meals a day and a roof over their heads. The athletes were captivated by the team's showcase schedule of games on national networks and cable television. They were charmed by the first class travel across the country with accommodations at luxurious hotels and meals at classy restaurants. And for the ultimate affirmation of big-time college basketball, many athletes spoke with great pride and emotion of playing in the NCAA tournament. They attempted to describe what is to them indescribable, a dream come true. Eventually, words such as "great" or "cool" are the best adjectives these athletes could share about their experience of competing in the NCAA tournament.

Yet probably the most seductive and overwhelming aspect of big time college basketball in the mindset of the Black athlete is the popularity and preferential treatment he received from other people on campus that follow the sport and seek to enhance their status by an association with him.

There are two societies at predominately White colleges with two opposite viewpoints on having the Black athlete on campus. The sports culture on campus is fascinated and enamored with the Black athlete. The academic culture is resentful and disturbed by the presence of the Black athlete on campus. They do not want an association with the Black athlete and grudgingly tolerate the necessary business relationship of sports and money. At most major universities the sports infrastructure is so defined that the Black athlete is often insulated from the segment of the university that is resentful of his stay. However, at smaller universities in Divisions I, II, and III, the athletes must make wise decisions to stay out of harm's way and confrontational situations.

For the Black athlete whose life off the court has generally been filled with disappointment, poverty, oppression, and invisibility, the prospect of celebrity status in the White community is irresistible and addictive. Unfortunately, the Black athlete fails to understand that his popular and kingly status—just as it was in his home environment—is tied to jump shots and not to his personal being.

Meanwhile, new communities of mostly White well-wishers, backslappers, and basketball groupies with their own subjective agendas snuggle up to support and showcase the Black athlete. The list of people attracted to Black athletes is extensive and diverse ranging from alumni and boosters to professors and women. Local politicians, community leaders, and school administrators all enjoy frivolous and brief encounters with the Black athlete. The requirements for the athletes are varied and are treated as goodwill relations and positive marketing by the university. They can include signing autographs for a children's group attending a game or visiting a local hospital for sick children. Some athletes have given private basketball clinics to children of a Dean or other top school officer. Under the guise of public relations, these types of ventures are necessary and understandable.

However, it is the people that are infatuated with the mystique of the athlete, and particularly the Black athlete, that pose the most uncertainty. Many Black former college athletes boast of fellow students who handled their class assignments and homework, or "loaned" them money or their cars simply for an association or connection to the athlete. They speak of the accessibility and ease of relationships with women, especially White women, a new situation most had never known considering their backgrounds. Many former athletes also speak of the generosity of adults in the sporting community that made their homes and families available to them. They were kind people from mostly well-to-do backgrounds that the athletes knew they could come to if they were in trouble or in need of anything. Seemingly, the only connection these concerned folks wanted was an identity and association with a winning program and its athletes. In essence, all the accolades and trappings of big time college basketball portray an athletic cocoon of sports dreams and comfort that the Black athlete enjoys, but never questions. This in turn leads to a diminished attempt and desire by the athlete to focus on getting his degree, forfeited for a continued false sense of security that the life of a star athlete is real and will proceed indefinitely.

However, the overall atmosphere of high society basketball for the Black athlete on White campuses is often no more than a controlled, military-like environment. A former major college head coach agrees, saying that, "Kids coming from the inner city generally have their classes, tutors, meals, and practices structured. They are not taught how to adjust, develop social skills, and understand the importance of planning and seeing a future outside of basketball. Their regimen is strictly basketball. They believe everything will be taken care of for them for the next four years because the coach told them so during the recruiting process. The coach made promises to take care of the kids, help them stay eligible and graduate, give them playing time, and ensure that they will get a good well-paying job after college because of the coach's contacts and connections. Consequently, the athlete believes he only has to play ball and everything will be taken care of. He does not see the need to develop socially, intellectually, or expand his horizons outside of sports."

So for many Black athletes after their athletic eligibility has expired, the realization occurs that the college experience was an "all that glitters is not gold" syndrome. When I questioned these athletes about their academic shortcomings, they admit they only did enough work to stay eligible to play ball. They say they did not understand that staying eligible and graduating in four years are and different scenarios. The NCAA requires an athlete to pass 24 semester credits each year and be in "good academic standing" as determined by their university. However, passing 24 credits each year totals only 96 credits after four years and most undergraduate programs require over 120 credits to graduate. Consequently, an athlete can stay eligible to compete for four years, but will fall short of graduating by a minimum of 24 credits (or a complete year) if he or she is not cognizant of the course load required and does not understand the importance of taking classes in the summers.

When I asked the athletes if their coach, tutors or academic advisors were ever concerned about their academic progress, most simply said, "No", as if they did not expect any support from the coach or his staff. Most athletes stated that as long as they remained eligible grades were never discussed. Interestingly, many of the athletes took the blame for their lack of academic progress admitting that all the trappings of being a star athlete headed for the NBA blinded them.

I asked the athletes if they were aware of the financial success of the coach and the school. A former ACC standout told me, "You see the million dollar contract for the coach and all the money the school gets but unless you are the star player guaranteed of going to the league [NBA] you have to keep quiet. Because if you want to get to the league you don't want to be labeled as a troublemaker with a negative attitude. So you just keep quiet."

Another disturbing theme that seemed to repeat itself during conversations with various Black college athletes was how their coach knew the X's and O's of coaching, but was "not a nice or good person" in their estimation. Most of these same athletes said they would not seek out any contact or relationship with the coach in the future. Many said they simply do not think any relationship with the coach or any help he could provide as a reference or go-between would be sincere. Knowing the importance of contacts and networking in the business world, I felt sorry for the athletes. Many of these athletes were instrumental to the athletic and financial success of the school and coach. But now, just a few short years removed from college, without their degrees and feeling shunned by their coach the only redeeming value of their college experience that could enhance their futures was the pride and memories of the games they played.

Conversely, a former ACC player told me how envious he was of the relationship between the former players at ACC schools such as Duke and North Carolina. The athlete stated, "The family relationship between past players and the school is not hype. It is real. They are a family and they network and the players stay in contact with each other, the school, and the coaches." I spoke to John Smith, a Black basketball athlete who graduated from Duke University in 1989, and he agreed. Smith said, "I could call Coach [Mike] Krzyzewski today and he would accept my call and would sincerely help if he could." However, clearly this situation is the exception to the rule. My interviews and conversations with players, combined with the NCAA statistics that three out of every four Black basketball athletes will leave college without a degree, is reflective of a short-term, employer-employee, business agreement rather than a teacher-student relationship between coach and player. While the athletic departments and the athlete should share equal share blame for the poor graduation rates, public sentiment seems to sympathize with the coach and school. It is a public relations situation of which most schools and college coaches take full advantage.

That Black athletes leave college after four and five years without degrees while having fortified and supplemented the school and coach's financial coffers and provided public goodwill and marketing through their athletic efforts is despicable. The athletes should rightfully shoulder much of the blame for their lack of a diploma. However, to feel wary of contacting their coach or university athletic administration for a referral or reference is a complete travesty.

What is truly sad is that nobody really seems to care. Most adults, both Black and White, that I interviewed apparently agree with the Black athlete that his failure to graduate is his decision and responsibility. Nevertheless, it is incredible to me that adults from 35-50 years of age that struggle daily with issues of self-discipline and focus place the blame exclusively on Black athletes 18-22 years old when they fail to maintain their balance and do not get their degrees while in college.

Then again, we should not expect an understanding or connection with the plight of the Black athlete from White society. The fact that three out of every four Black athletes fail to graduate is not directly their problem. On the other hand, any Black man or women that enjoys college basketball, makes it a priority to follow "March Madness" and the NCAA tournament, but does nothing to educate our youth about the importance of taking advantage of an opportunity to get a college education is a hypocrite. Our silence except to cheer after every basket only confirms to the colleges and the Black athletes that sport and winning are more important than their development, and education as Black men and women.

Why Black Athletes Fail to Graduate from College

* Returning Home From College *

The NBA draft has come and gone. The college athletic career is over. Your college class has worn its cap and gown and marched across the stage in May. You aren't sure what your academic classification is or even how many credits you need to graduate. It does not matter anyway. You have never thought of being anything else but a professional basketball player. Now what?

A great deal of Black players return home to the Black community without their degrees but with stories to tell of how "things just didn't work out," about how the "system" or "program" was against them despite their efforts. It garners understanding and support for the self-fulfilling prophesy of how you can't beat the "White man" at his own game when playing with a stacked deck. This is a typical battle cry and knee-jerk refrain used by a segment of the Black community. But at least the athlete gets "props" for trying. And everybody knows that the athlete "got game" and because of that obvious fact, it truly was the "system" and not his fault. After all, when the talented athlete left for college a few years ago he was the latest "best player to come out of the city since…"

Do not criticize the Black athlete for wanting to reach the highest plateau the sport has to offer. The NBA dream is what sustained him to reach the college level. But the fault does lie with the athlete when he totally sells out in order to play the sport's next level and forfeits his college education in the process. And why criticize just the athlete? A whole lot of people led him and failed him on his path to becoming a hooked on hoops athlete. Start with the coaches that recruited the player and the universities that sapped him of his physical gifts for a Final Four financial bonanza. The Black neighborhoods that encouraged him to play for the predominately White university without the proper preparation and mental outlook should also be held accountable. And let's include the athlete himself with his one dimensional, NBA only focus. All share the blame for his lack of a college degree. What's worse, now home again in the Black sports culture, the athlete's absence of a degree is deemed business as usual. Everybody seems to be indifferent instead of indignant. Perhaps we see ourselves the way some colleges see us after all; as athletic "hired guns" on a temporary mission. Or perhaps we have been brainwashed into believing the system of college sports is too big and that we are powerless to take it on except to make it to the NBA.

When our Black athletes return home without their degrees, we give them a pat on the back for attempting to take on the "man's" system, but console them and ourselves with the belief that they were up against long odds. We give credence to the excuse that the coach lied to the player and the community. And now we want to believe that the coach and university never really cared about helping the player anyway. Sadly, the athlete enhances this proposition with excuses as to why "things just didn't work out." In fact, he discusses his lack of an NBA opportunity more so than he does missing his degree, almost as though graduation was never a real priority.

The Black athlete returns to the neighborhood displaying a watch from the NCAA tournament and reminiscing about why he never received the NBA chance he knew was meant for him. Always it is how something seemed to go wrong that was beyond his control. The Black athlete's excuse book features the same alibis each year. "The 'man' didn't like my style." " The coach wanted a White player to get all the shots." "The coach's style didn't fit my game and our personalities clashed." " I injured my knee and the coach never let me get my position back." But these are basketball excuses.

What went wrong in the classroom? The conversation never comes up, because getting a degree was never a real goal in the first place. It was part of the hustle just to get into school and chase the NBA dream. Consequently, when his basketball career went bad his schoolwork, never of great interest anyway, followed suit. Many Black athletes that are hooked on hoops only to return home again believe that a professional shot is still a strong possibility. They speak of pro summer leagues and semi-pro tryouts and "connections" that will provide them with a chance to play with a team in Europe. But until that happens, if that happens, (and it usually does not) they search for a job, one that they never thought they would have to settle for when they left the same community several years ago as an athletic King of the Hill.

Many Black athletes have a more difficult time adjusting to the sudden impact of being outside of the athletic limelight than they do to the lack of a college degree. They simply never thought the ball would stop bouncing, especially at the age of 22. They did not comprehend the premise that the spotlight would fade to black, the athletic curtain would fall, and the applause would cease. The abruptness and finality of the end of a college athletic career combined with a now non-existent NBA chance is a jolt to the system of many Black athletes. After a dozen years of star status and special treatment the Black athlete often is ill-prepared for the next step in his life. He has not provided for his future away from basketball and, confused about his outlook, he still seeks the rush provided by competition and adulation. Sure, the Black community and Black sports culture rightfully accepts the athlete home, but this attention is focused on the next basketball prodigy. It will assist the athlete in getting on his feet with possible job opportunities and other endeavors and the athlete will reciprocate by playing ball and keeping his athletic legacy alive. Yet, it is a melancholy portrait of wasted potential and low expectations. So much more should occur. In fact, just the opposite should occur.

Many of our nation's universities do an outstanding job of getting the Black athlete to graduate. And, contrary to public perception that books and successful teams don't mix, these schools graduate athletes while maintaining top flight, winning programs. Michigan State University basketball coached by Tom Izzo went to three straight Final Fours (1999-2001), won the National

Championship in 2000 and still graduated all five Black athletes that were seniors on the 2001 team. Other major basketball-power universities that have had success graduating the Black athlete include Duke, North Carolina, Georgetown, Notre Dame, Indiana, Penn St., Northwestern, Fordham, George Washington, Dayton, Xavier, and Stanford.

However, pure statistics are deceiving. Even schools, with the best of intentions find it difficult to graduate players that come to campus hooked on hoops, with academic shortcomings who transfer or leave early for the NBA. Just as many or more schools have cursory goals of graduating Black players, and have a long and consistent track record of failing to do so. These schools need to be exposed. The best sources to highlight them are the former athletes, themselves, who did not graduate from these particular schools. If these Black athletes speak to young, up and coming recruits during the recruiting process, perhaps they will sign with competing schools that graduate their players. Once the failing schools lose recruits and games to colleges that graduate players, change will occur, starting with the firing of hypocritical and phony coaches. The only way to go after the big college programs that continually exploit our athletes is to cut off their primary source of power; the talented Black athlete from our communities.

* Improving Black Athlete's Graduation Rates *

The melancholy story repeated so many times by so many Black athletes does not have to continue. Change may not come overnight, but it can happen. First, our Black sports culture needs to fortify our young athletes with an understanding of self beyond basketball, the importance of ethnic value, and a knowledge of our history, especially as it pertains to the value of education. This must occur both before the athletes sign with a college and jointly with the praise and pride we have for their athletic accomplishments and

NBA future. The Black community should provide information to the parents and young stars about the academics of the schools trying to recruit them. Parents need to make it a priority to seek out information from recruiters and the NCAA about the graduation rate of Black athletes. Unfortunately, many parents, ask more questions about the NBA and paydays than they do about graduation rates. They must look the coach or assistant coach straight in the eye and ask, "What is the graduation rate of Black athletes at your school? In the basketball program?"

Secondly, we need to instill in our young Black athletes a different perspective concerning the purpose of a college scholarship. Our mindset of college must go beyond the euphoria of receiving a scholarship and believing our young athlete is on the fast track to a professional career. We must adopt the mental framework that a college degree is the ultimate goal.

The Black athlete must understand that getting a college degree and pursuing a professional career can be simultaneous goals. The athlete does not have to choose one or the other and indeed, both are within his grasp. In the eyes of most Black athletes that are hooked on hoops, anything less than a professional career is considered coming up short of the dream. It is a misconception that needs to be stricken from the rationale of the Black athlete in the big city. A 10,000 to 1 shot to play professional sports should not be a goal to strive for without a counterbalance or alternative plan of action. A blueprint is needed that must include a college degree.

For the athlete fortunate enough to garner an athletic scholarship, his attitude should be to work on his craft and continue to be the best athlete he can be. But he must expend the same amount of energy to receive his college degree.

When the Black athlete moves on to college he must become multi-faceted in all walks of his life and not one dimensional, solely dependent on basketball. True, he must always continue to work on his athletic skills to maintain his scholarship because it is what sent him to college and should never be compromised. Also, the Black athlete will always believe that a professional career is on his horizon and nobody should dissuade him from this assessment. But hopefully, with the exposure and maturity gained from his college experience he can come to visualize that a degree is the ultimate goal whether a professional sports career is realized or not. It is a difficult test for the Black athlete to untangle the confusing puzzle of his professional sports dreams, his commitment to his people and community, the obligations of his scholarship and the value of a college degree. But change must happen and the Black athlete is in a prime position to press for action.

No longer should we tolerate three Black athletes out of every four attending college on a basketball scholarship to return home without a degree. The Black community must teach its youth the principles which will prepare them for the value of a degree before they go to college. Clearly understand that if it were three out of four White athletes returning home without their degrees the White community would be up in arms and excuses would not be tolerated. Their alarm and outrage would result in major reforms within collegiate sports including the immediate dismissal of college coaches with paltry graduation rates.

There are four indisputable facts regarding the Black scholarship athlete at predominately White Division I colleges:

* **First.** Most Black basketball athletes do not graduate.

* **Second.** The athletic department in particular and the university community apparently will not even hire the Black athletes that do graduate. The 1998 Racial and Gender Report Card presented by Northeastern University's Center for the Study of Sport in Society supports the theory.

In 1997-98, of jobs that are classified as front office/manage-ment such as compliance coordinators, agents, sports information director or assistant athletic director, Black men held only six percent of the positions while Black females held only three percent. These are solid career opportunities that can lead to advancement within the athletic department to other prestigious positions. However, with such low Black representation in these positions the pipeline of qualified Black candidates is low and consequently Blacks do not advance.

* **Third.** Many universities and their athletic departments and coaches with large paychecks and lavish public acclaim, will eagerly await another promising crop of Black athletes for the upcoming season. They alternately deflect blame for the eventual poor graduation rates to the players' own lackadaisical efforts, ill prepared high school academic backgrounds, and NBA obsessed attitudes.

* **Fourth.** Help, with only a few exceptions such as The National Consortium for Academics and Sports (NCAS), must come from within our own communities. We should not rely on the NCAA or the NBA to solve what most believe is our problem.

The National Consortium for Academics and Sports was established by Northeastern University's Center for the Study of Sport in Society in 1985 to help create a better society by focusing on educational attainment and using the power and appeal of sport to affect social change. The NCAS evolved in response to the need to "keep the student in student-athlete." The goal of the NCAS and its member institutions is to bring back, tuition free, their own former student-athletes who competed in revenue sports and were unable to complete their degree requirements. In exchange for this honor and opportunity, these former student-athletes participate in school outreach and community service programs. The NCAS is having great success. Since 1985, when the program started with just 11 colleges and universities participating, more than 21,978 student-athletes have returned to school to complete their degrees. As of the summer of 2001, 8,625 of these former student-athletes have graduated. Meanwhile, the NCAS has increased its membership to 215 colleges and universities.

Substantial change will only take place when the Black community becomes self-reliant and determined to help itself. What is needed is a new attitude and sense of value of what a college education is worth. The Black community must teach our young Black athletes to have multiple dreams and goals. It is okay to dream of a professional sports career, but it is just as important to dream of a college degree. It can never be taken away from you. Above all, our Black athletes should dream of self-empowerment and lifting their people. It is God's purpose. Do not limit your aspirations. Don't box yourself into one corner or the other. Have the goal to accomplish them all.

* Infiltrate, Graduate, and Infiltrate *

Currently, the Black athlete knows the path to the NBA and what it entails. Though he understands the route to graduate, application is often lacking. What he does not know is the principle of "infiltrate, graduate, and infiltrate." This rule of conduct outlines how the black community and black athlete can understand, visualize, value and take advantage of the opportunity for higher education at colleges and universities. Scholarship athletes, specifically, must grasp this principle. Their athletic gift has provided them an inroad to college where their education is paid. They, above all others must seize this tremendous opportunity to become more than an athlete but a beacon for future success in any avenue of life.

The first step in the principle is acquiring and gathering information for our personal and community betterment. Our Black

Why Black Athletes Fail to Graduate from College

athletes need to infiltrate the college environment to learn and extract every bit of information they can grasp with the idea of establishing independence for himself and his community. This acquisition of knowledge should extend beyond the basketball court and even the classroom to include the entire college experience.

The second step in the principle is for the athlete to graduate. Supposedly, this has always been a goal but was never fulfilled. Perhaps if our Black athletes are approached about the reasons for a college degree in terms of self-empowerment, community leadership, and self-reliance instead of merely enabling him to get a "good" job, it will initiate a different attitude. Our Black athletes have become sought after stars on the basketball court because of their intelligence, creativity and courage to take chances to excel when pressure inhibits other players. So it would stand to reason that they are not opposed to leadership and have an independent and take charge spirit. Just maybe, the concept of asking our high performance, goal oriented, Black athletes to get a college degree just to settle for a loosely projected, nondescript job is a devaluation and misinterpretation of what motivates him. In fact, could it be that the Black community's own low expectations of what entails a good job (remember when our goal was always to get a good government paying position?) insults the Black athlete and intensifies his pursuit of a professional career?

Graduation provides the credentials necessary to open doors in the workplace. It legitimizes any endeavor the Black athlete may want to pursue and it provides access and mobility in predominately White corporate America. In 2001, 98 percent of all Blacks in America worked for White people. Therefore, when the Black athlete goes to work after graduation, a White business owner will probably sign his paycheck. It is merely the economic face of our country but it can change in the future. It is also why the Black athlete must seize the fantastic and blessed opportunity provided by a college athletic scholarship to college. It is why the Black athlete should infiltrate and grasp his total college experience.

Graduation also provides for the third step of the principle. Upon entering the working stream of corporate America, the Black athlete must again infiltrate a new environment. Just as in college, he must learn all that he can from the business community. Just as in college he must mingle, converse, listen to and learn all aspects of the business environment. He must understand his job assignment, because like his college scholarship it must never be compromised. But he should also learn other assignments and other positions within the organization.

When the three-step principle is complete, the Black athlete is ready to better himself and improve his community. He has been taught well and through his ability to infiltrate, graduate, and infiltrate, he has the confidence, methodology, and knowledge to produce positive winning results. As exemplified by his multiple basketball skills, he never lacked heart, imagination or desire. Now he has the direction.

The results can have a positive domino effect. A community that once felt powerless to stem the tide of athletes returning home without their college degrees now has a positive role model and knowledgeable leader for improvement. The Black athlete returning from college without his degree but rightfully knowing that he will be welcomed back home with love now returns with ideas instead of excuses. And most important, our future Black athletes have a tangible and positive role model to emulate.

* How to Infiltrate *

Black athletes need to head to college with the mindset to learn as much as they can, about as many things as they can and meet as many people as they can. Black athletes must participate in as many endeavors as they can. Our objective should become to infiltrate the college environment. One thing about playing basketball at the collegiate level, especially in Division I, is that it accords the

Why Black Athletes Fail to Graduate from College

Black athlete great access to a multitude of people and exposure to different venues. Athletes get to travel across the country and see other cultures and ways that people interact. People from various walks of life want to bond and associate with the athlete. These opportunities should not be taken casually and these should be considered learning tools to be extracted for future reference. There is so much more to the college experience, than just books, tests, practices, and games. True, these are what will ultimately help you graduate and should be a priority. But solely eliciting books and basketball from the college experience is shortsighted and deprives yourself, your future, and your community of valuable and life-sustaining lessons. Black athletes need to go to college to learn how things are done, how business is conducted, how networks are formed, and how relationships are initiated and bonded.

Since the Black scholarship athlete on scholarship is such a valuable commodity to the university, he has inside privilege and access to information on how business is conducted. He has an opportunity to get up close and personal to witness how White people operate and function. It is a chance that in all probability will never occur again.

The athlete has opportunities to attend fundraising activities within the athlete department and on campus. They have chances to learn about business while lending support to positive endeavors like Special Olympics and other non-profit and charitable ventures. They have occasion to meet booster clubs, alumni groups and local community sponsors such as car dealerships and restaurant owners. There are chances to help other sports such as volleyball, tennis and soccer. In the athletic offices, administrative staff and secretaries enjoy conversations and exchanging ideas with the athletes. The television and radio personnel, always looking for information that will make them seem "in the know" to their viewers and listeners, can never have enough dialogs with athletes. Indeed, the opportunities for the Black athlete to meet different people and learn how business affairs are facilitated and relationships are shaped are numerous.

The Black athlete should be sincere, humble, inquisitive and outgoing. He should be honest and caring about his fellow man. Gathering information for a better goal and a better way for yourself and your community is called ambition. Yet it does not require devious and deceitful deportment. Infiltration is not about trickery and lies. In fact, the principle of Infiltrate, Graduate, Infiltrate is a vehicle for self-reliance leading to self-empowerment. It is a long-term course of action requiring our community and our athletes to understand the vastness of the scholarship opportunity accorded them.

CHAPTER THIRTEEN:
Attitudes and Perceptions of Sports
within the Black Community

If a new attitude is to surface for our Black athletes to take full advantage of going to college on an athletic scholarship, an alliance has to form between all aspects of Black society. For our talented athletes with multiple skills and gifts to really understand the importance of going to college and having their education paid for requires a team approach. Right now within the Black community this is not possible because the sentiments of the group that see the benefits of sport is just as strong as the assembly that resents and opposes athletics. The Black community is divided into these two distinct outlooks on sports and sports participation by our youth. Only when the Black community takes part in an analysis of sports with a critical eye and understands both the positives and the overindulgence of sports will a change occur to stem the tide of corruption and abuse of our young Black athletes. Until then, the multi-billion dollar industry of sports with its unquenchable appetite will continue to feast on the youth of the Black community.

A quick consensus must be reached within the Black community regarding sports and our youth, lest we lose our most precious resource, our children, to fulfill someone else's dreams while alternately continuing our nightmare of exploitation. Participants in the debate on the impact of sports in our community acknowledge two things. First, sports can lead to a college education and second, sports are a fixture in our community and nation.

One group would agree that sports have captured not only our youth, but their parents and a large portion of our community. They feel that our young athletes are walking athletic zombies with a trance-like fixation on sports combined with a totally unrealistic and misplaced value system concerning what sports can do for them. This group can be defined as pragmatic.

171

Pragmatists feel that our youth should do other things, seek other interests in life and strive to be something other than an athlete. They agree with Charles Barkley's statement that professional athletes are not role models. They feel that there is a total overemphasis on trying to become an athlete and what it means to be an athlete. They are mystified by the Black culture's lionization of the athlete. They readily point to the dismal statistics of college graduation rates and the long shot chance of playing professionally as examples of how Black youth waste valuable years of their lives chasing a fool's gold dream that just will not happen. Pragmatists go on talk shows, forums, seminars, and other speaking engagements, and tell all that our Black youth should not dream of becoming Michael Jordan.

In theory, it is a no-brainer. There is only one Michael Jordan and the odds of playing professional sports is 1 in 10,000. Nobody can dispute the tremendous odds of a professional sports career. But the issue becomes what and how do you replace the goals of the youth if you crush the dream of sports. Their next sentence, after emphasising the dismal odds of a professional career, is never about what careers youth should pursue or how to get them interested if one is suggested. Their rhetoric offers no answer as to how to break the fixation that the Black community has with sports and athletes.

It is such an oversimplification of the problem that many people in the sports community wonder about a possible hidden agenda of the speaker. Consequently, to the Black youth they want to save, they appear to have an elitist, ivory-tower, approach youth can smell as phony and insincere from miles away. At the least, many of the youth believe the speaker is out of touch with the real issues facing Black youth in the big city.

First and foremost, any dream, vision, goal or achievement by a Black youth should be applauded, encouraged and sincerely endorsed. Black youth, especially those raised poor, are deluged with problems, stereotypes and other issues just by being born Black. Studies reveal that young Black boys generally start having problems or become disinterested in school between the second and fourth grades. Many Black youth start losing hope for a better day by age 16 or 17. Still others start seriously talking about their mortality as early as 21. Therefore, any goal or dream, especially one that entails work, and dedication, and definitely education, should be applauded. Regardless of the odds of a professional sports career, the fact that Black youth have a dream is an accomplishment. Nobody has a right to dash the dream. Educate them on the probabilities and percentages of the success of a professional sports career, but never attempt to crush their dream.

I was in attendance at a Rainbow/Push Wall Street Project Sports Forum in the summer of 1999 when David Aldridge, now the NBA analyst for ESPN, was a guest speaker. Aldridge, a local product from northeast Washington DC, told the audience that while speaking to a fifth grade class in Washington DC he asked how many students dreamed of playing professional basketball. After most of the boys raised their hands, he told them to forget about that dream and think of something else. Later, when asked by the teacher of the class why he crushed the dreams of the young Black students, Aldridge said, "The kids needed to know the truth now, rather than later." Who made him clairvoyant? What would have happened if a professional came to his classroom while at Taft Junior High School and told him to forget any idea of becoming a Black journalist or sports reporter?

Nobody has a right to force their will and supposed expertise on a youth's dream because they think they know what is best. This is especially true for Black youth who often experience more pain and despair than joy and success in their lives. If you can't find it in your heart to co-sign the professional sports career, then encourage the positives of having a dream and teach that the mind is capable of having multiple dreams, and the spirit and body is capable of reaching them all. Inherent in the dream of a NBA career are positive attributes including hard work, dedication, commitment, goal-setting, teamwork, resiliency, discipline, and hope.

The other group is the Black sports community. This group believes that sports are beneficial to the community and athlete. Granted, they will say that many young athletes and parents lose perspective of the relevance of sports, but they basically see the positives that sports teach our youth. They understand how the teachings of sports can benefit young athletes. They recite that although a dream of becoming a professional athlete is a long shot, it is a dream that entails striving for success, hard work, and dedication. The dream spawns positive influences along the way such as having good grades and attending college. In Black communities filled with blight and despair, sports are a positive force. In fact, they will say that it is not the professional sports dream that is the problem, but rather the lack of having multiple dreams.

Interestingly, both groups, the pragmatist and the sports community, agree that there is an overemphasis on sports in the Black community. They both concur that the odds are too long for youth to dream exclusively of a professional sports career, yet both are short on ideas about how to generate interest in new and different dreams. They both agree that sports is here to stay, with the exposure and profits and exploitation of our youth becoming more brazen and pressure-packed each season while starting with younger athletes each year. The debate centers on the relative value of sports in the process. The pragmatist says why waste the time and energy when sports will ultimately leave the Black youth exploited and ineffective. The sports community, on the other hand promotes the life skills generated through sports that will keep the youth out of harm's way and assist them later as adults.

Perhaps the biggest difference between the groups is social class and whether sports were ever played competitively and seen as a valuable contribution to their life and success. People that have reached a certain social level without participation in sports are a lot less tolerant and more skeptical of the meaning and value of sports than are former athletes. As a member of the sports community and a former athlete, I am committed to the positive and life enhancing values learned from sports participation and competition.

To formulate a new attitude for our Black youth, we must expand our efforts beyond the understanding of sports and competition. We need the renewed commitment of the Black professional that once called the Black community home. The Black professional has not only misplaced his identity and association with the city, but has become skeptical and distrustful of Black people in general and the Black male specifically. This attitude and perception must be re-examined and ultimately changed.

A good friend and former teammate, Steve Dyer, asked me with amazement how I could dare go into some of the tough neighborhoods such as Anacostia in far southeast and officiate games. He was curious if I was scared and fearful for my safety. The implication was that I was foolish; what was the value of putting myself in harm's way by venturing into the big city. I was, in turn, incredulous of his statement. For perspective, as a Black man I am more fearful of being pulled over by county police late at night coming home after the game than I am officiating the game. Here was a Black man telling me that I should be afraid of Black boys that looked like me and it was not just any Black man, but a former high school and college athlete that was raised in the big city and learned his athletic craft on the rough and tumble city playgrounds. I do understand Steve's question. I just did not expect it to come from a Black man who I thought would understand and be sympathetic to the plight of the Black male and Black athlete.

The more pressing concern is, if a Black athlete raised on hoops can have a fearful and distrusting attitude toward Black males and Black athletes, then what negative thoughts, disproportionate stereotypes, and impulsive fears must other people, both Black and

White have? For example, what perceptions and ideals do White suburbanites have who are without a first hand experience with the Black male or Black athlete? Without first hand knowledge, their opinions are formulated strictly by newspaper, radio, and television accounts of Black life which, without a proper balance, would seem to leave them wondering what type of anarchy is taking place. If your only identity of Black life is from the News at 11, or from the Metro section of the newspaper, then you are not receiving a positive or balanced account of life in the city. Favorable or optimistic stories about the Black community rarely make the news. The media, dominated by folks of other races, generally prefers to promote Blacks as the frontrunners of our societal ills, rather than highlight our virtues and non-athletic accomplishments.

It is one thing for White society to be fearful of our Black youth, especially males, and to stereotype our Black athletes for they don't know better, and they cannot identify with our lifestyle or our plight. However, it is a shameful indictment of Black divisiveness when Black folk, raised in the Black community and totally aware of the problems, turn away and lose sight of where they came from. Sadly, many Blacks are quite content in not wanting to remember and merely lock the gates of their castles and live life through their remote control.

The Black professional who has left the community cannot bury his head in the sand to ignore the plight of Black folk. Moving to the suburbs and achieving financial status does not change anyone's skin color. As long as the negatives and unflattering stereotypical images emanating from the media are the primary reference point for White folks, the suburban and affluent Black will never fully be trusted and accepted as an equal in White society. Marcus Franklin, a columnist for the *Detroit Free Press* once wrote, "Each Black man pays in ways big and small for any misdeeds of the other 16,562,999 Black men in this nation."

The adage that a chain is only as strong as its weakest link applies to the struggle of the Black man in this country. The Black professional that has overcome hardships to meet financial and alleged social status is a valuable instrument to generate leadership, impart knowledge, set high standards and provide a tangible reference point of productivity and self-empowerment. He or she can force change, and create a different attitude in the Black community. It is simple math to comprehend that you can not ask youth to shun deviant behavior or suggest that athletes create other dreams without showing them established and successful Black men and women as examples of such dreams. Youth deal in actions and visualizations not abstracts. The Black community lacks discernible examples of Black success.

Meanwhile, Black youth see the lack of adult guidance, participation and supervision. When youth sense community apathy, suspicion, disrespect, and fear, the ramifications include crime, drug abuse, and violent behavior. For many youth, an over-concentration on sports such as basketball is viewed as one of the few positive approaches to get attention and to be seen.

When Black professionals and Black folk in general move from the Black community to the suburbs, many aspects of Black life are forsaken. First and foremost is our personal connection with our disadvantaged and disenfranchised brothers who remain in the Black community. Just as prominent is the division formed between our youth leading to total miscommunication over what problems they are dealing with and what is on their mind. Then, with our hectic lifestyles in order to keep pace with the "things" we have acquired relative to being successful in suburbia, we allow other information-gathering sources to tell us about us. Often, the story told by these media outlets, including news organizations, television programs, movies, sports events and highlight shows, is not a balanced depiction of Black life.

But since we are far too busy to critically analyze what we watch, especially in sports, where we just want athletic drama to unfold and provide us with an entertaining diversion, we generally yield to another group's interpretation of our lifestyle. For example in the 1999-2000 season in the three major professional sports, the NBA, NFL, and Major League Baseball, Blacks held only 16 percent, 2 percent, and 4 percent, respectively, of the radio and television announcers positions. Unknowingly we watch, listen, and accept the stereotypes expressed by these announcers who tell us that "basketball saved this athlete's life," or "saved him from jail" or how sports helped this Black athlete to "escape" his rough environment. And while sports may have provided an opportunity, the repetitiveness of these stories, especially for Black athletes, leads one to believe that only the Black athlete with his physical gifts (there is no mention of intellectual capabilities, or willpower or self-discipline) can make it out of his surroundings through sports. The redundant cliches are offensive and disparaging, and constrain Black achievement and the advancement of our culture.

Are we really predestined for jail unless we can dunk a basketball? Of course not! Yet these subtle, overused, and inhibiting references are repeatedly applied to Black athletes by mostly White announcers. They go unchecked and unquestioned by the Black community.

The general exclusion of Blacks by the mainstream media, combined with our apathy towards forming an allegiance to deal with the concerns of our youth, leaves us exposed to another group's interpretations, standards, and guidelines of our lifestyle. Consequently, when the Black community does not meet the standards set forth by others, we are portrayed negatively. The Black community, often divided, unsure, and unmotivated to question the information and its source concurs with the media's representation of our lifestyle, instead of seeking clarity. As a result, the stereotypes and generally negative portrayal become our standard and we accept pessimistic images of our own people. If we only showed a greater tenacity and concern for our own, we would find a different, yet resilient Black community positively marching forward.

Attitudes and Perceptions of Sports within the Black Community

I went to officiate a high school basketball game in the city at Phelps Vocational High School located in the Benning Road corridor of northeast Washington DC. It was a typical mid-week seven pm start, normal for most high school games in Washington DC. To get to the gym from the parking lot required walking through several hallways. As I walked toward the gym and peered into the classrooms I was overjoyed to see that almost every classroom was filled with Black students reading books and manuals, writing down assignments and participating in group discussions. Not only were students from the school at work, but adults, men and women, and senior citizens were all joined together to learn and better themselves. It was uplifting to see so many adults in a rough area of town out in the cold and dark winter night in pursuit of knowledge and self-improvement.

My euphoria continued as I refereed a spirited and competitive game between two good high school basketball teams. The crowd was enthusiastic but controlled and the players competed with intensity and sportsmanship. The coaches were teaching and encouraged the athletes' efforts on the floor. As I left the gym around 10 o'clock and passed the same classrooms as I had three hours prior, many were still filled with students. I was full of pride and a sense of accomplishment over the positive community effort I saw from youth at a ballgame and adults in classrooms, especially in an area of town lacking in optimism and viable options.

The following morning I anxiously opened the paper to get a recap of the game and was immediately hit by the headline of a slain body dumped on the street only a block from the school. Naturally, that was the attention-grabbing headline. It seemed to me that the newspaper's account made specific and repeated references to the four public schools, that share the same block. It was as if they tried to link the incident with these institutions. Or at least make parents fearful of sending their kids to school. Once again, a tragedy overshadowed a community's positive experience.

179

I can recall having game assignments at other Washington DC schools and seeing similar positive examples of quiet perseverance and self-improvement. At Ballou Senior High School, in far southeast Washington, I always saw a different setting than what the newspapers would report. Ballou High School is in a section of town that if you do not have relatives in the area, then the joke is that you do not belong there. The traffic dynamics are such that the area does not provide a shortcut to get to a major thoroughfare or easy access out of town or to the business district downtown. So, unless visiting relatives or living in the area "street talk" would say you should not be in the neighborhood.

However, I enjoyed game assignments at the high school and, having lived in the area briefly as a youngster, I was never fearful. What immediately struck me as I drove to the games, were the volumes of people getting off of public buses trying to get home from work. Many other residents of the area got off of the buses with grocery bags, shopping and laundry bags having completed errands. The neighborhood was bustling with the activity of hard working people attempting to complete their day and get a head start on tomorrow, no different than any other community. It was a far cry from the headlines that gave the perception that lawlessness and turmoil were the norms for this community.

At the school and game, there were many positive displays of pride, self-respect, and purpose. The gym had a new floor installed and the recently replaced lighting was bright and illuminating. The team had sparkling new uniforms, as did the prep band that played and marched in unison before the game, during time outs, at halftime, and at the conclusion of the game. Small things that make a clear start at creating change must begin with a positive attitude. In truth, the spirit and energy from the students, and the adult leadership and commitment from concerned coaches, school administrators and the local police rivals that of public and private schools in the more affluent suburbs.

Attitudes and Perceptions of Sports
within the Black Community

The experience was far different from the media portrayal of a crime ridden, drug infested community with poor, corrupt, immoral, and apathetic, Black people waiting for welfare or government assistance. What truly is bothersome is the number of Black folks that agree with the media's descriptions and accounts. It is clearly and distinctly a case of brainwashing and a lack of ethnic value. Yes, the community has an inordinate amount of problems that are real and must be addressed. But the overwhelming majority of the community consists of good, hard working, family-oriented people striving for a better day. It is no different than any other people in any other community in this country.

Interestingly, it was always other Black people who questioned me about what happens when I go into the Black community to work games. (Then again, perhaps Whites did not ask the question feeling that it had racial overtones.) They assumed that trouble had to follow because, after all, I was going into allegedly rough neighborhoods after dark by myself. I would often think that if Black folk lack ethnic value, and are this apprehensive and suspicious, how much self-respect do they really have for themselves. It stands to reason that if a Black man fails to see ethnic value in his brother, why would a White person, without any understanding of Black culture, be able to make a distinction and see ethnic value in him.

CHAPTER FOURTEEN:
Solutions for Changing the Future

A sense of urgency is needed in the Black community and Black sports culture of our nation. No longer can we watch sports inattentively and simply root for the home team, take pride in the number of Black athletes competing on the floor, and quietly wish every-day living were this cut-and-dry. In addition, we must stop believing that sports are independent of society, like some athletic theme park where we can come and go, choose which roller coasters we want to ride, have a good time and relive our youth while accepting no control over which new rides the park will have in the future. We have the potential, the capability, the expertise and the obligation to direct our young athletes toward a new attitude and relationship with sports and the importance of education, community, and self-empowerment. Achieving this goal starts with the direction and leadership of our youth off the court.

Community leaders say that many Black youth see just three avenues for financial success: drugs, sports, and music. This is a particular indictment of the lack of leadership and concrete examples of success provided by our Black professionals and college educated young leaders. If we do not provide adequate opportunities for our youth to see and strive for other employment, then we can not chastise them if they channel their energy, time, and dreams toward a sports career. In fact, not only are we promoting their fascination with a sports career, we are failing to generate a "second dream" of success when the sports dream inevitably dissipates. This sets our athletes up for a painful fall, one that will require community assistance to help them get up.

Any action must first start with a positive attitude,—a commitment to change started from the heart, soul, and mind. Once a positive attitude is in place a vision, direction and determination are set and then, we can pursue a course of action. If the Black community and the Black athlete are to put sports, particularly basketball, in its proper perspective we must show our youth substantive and tangible alternatives to success. Sports in this country is a multi-billion dollar industry. Yet, the greatest fallacy among Black youth is that their only way to participate in sports is to play the game.

The next time our youth attend a game, parents should try to put the hype of the game aside and go into the arena with a perspective that encompasses all the jobs and professions on display. They will find a lost treasure. Almost every employable opportunity involved with the athletic event will be dominated, enjoyed and serviced by the White community. It is not an indictment but a social fact. Once into the arena it is very easy to notice that perhaps nine of the ten players on the floor will be Black athletes, but generally in no other employment opportunity will you see the Black face as the central figure.

For Black youth in the big city, our concentration is far too heavy and narrowly-focused on being part of the game instead of being part of the sports industry. Too many times, the Black athlete and the Black community have sold out and misused educational opportunities in order to be part of the game and not the sport which offers a multitude of viable, discernable and rewarding careers. Our Black youth must be taught and exposed to alternatives to the belief that playing the game professionally is the only way to be successful. This can be accomplished without asking the youth to forfeit his dream of an athletic career. In fact, it can be illustrated to the youth that his dream of a professional sports career can help him to envision other careers, possibly within the sports industry. The goal is not to deflate a youth's dream, but to produce a "Second Dream."

If the youth is committed to becoming a professional basketball player, then at least we have a starting point of a hope and a desire to achieve. The opportunity is now in place to expand their base of interest. If the youth wants to be a basketball player he must love sports. The love can become the impetus to how he can stay close to the game off the court and after his playing career is over. Then through sports we can introduce him to other careers and opportunities that are available to him in the sporting industry.

Perhaps the easiest way to expose the youth to alternative careers is to sponsor field trips to professional or collegiate sporting events. But it has to be so much more than just seeing stars of the game score 25 points. It will require a joint effort by college and professional teams, stadium and arena management, schools, and recreation centers, and most important, parents and community leaders. Trips to sporting events can offer a chance for youth to see a large collection of careers and job opportunities. (In the Chicago Bulls Media Guide there is a listing of over 70 different jobs from administration to marketing to upper management that are necessary to conduct day-to-day business.) With a coordinated effort, youth can be bused to games approximately two or three hours before a game. Once inside the arena, they can be taken on a tour to see various jobs and careers that are available in the sports industry. They can watch television and radio engineers, technicians and production staff set up for the telecast and radio broadcast of the game. They can watch cameramen and women service their equipment and position themselves for the telecast.

They can watch sportscasters and announcers, public relations and technical staff prepare for the evening. They can see stadium and arena management coordinate the necessary events to ensure a safe and smooth transition for the crowd prior to a game. There are sportswriters, player agents, coaches, referees, medical staff and trainers, restaurant services personnel, salesmen, electricians, entrepreneurial vendors, and many more career opportunities that are on display to ensure a safe and positive event will happen for everyone in attendance.

Perhaps a few of these professionals can spend 10 to 15 minutes speaking with groups of youth to explain their careers and how they relate to sports. The idea is to illustrate to youth through their love of sports what other jobs and careers they can have that are still involved in sports, but are off the playing fields and courts. For a follow up, youth that express a desire to learn more about a specific career or job must be placed in contact with workshops, apprenticeships and internships that offer the training and teaching they need.

Black athletes in the Black communities should be taught the benefits of social and communication skills. The Black athlete does himself and his community a disservice when he cannot project and articulate his thoughts accurately. Stereotypes and misconceptions are reinforced when Black athletes mumble, stutter and stammer during interviews. It is very disconcerting to listen to sports talk radio on White stations and hear how our Black athletes and their quotes and interviews are mocked and disparaged. The same people that beg for an interview, autograph, or personal appearance and cheer enthusiastically at the games laugh and make light of Black slang and mispronounced words that reinforce their opinion that the Black athlete, although physically more gifted, is still mentally inferior.

To the contrary, our Black athletes are very bright, poised and quick-witted. Often, it is the unfamiliarity and uneasiness of having a room full of predominately White media, television cameras, and microphones shoved in their faces moments after the completion of an athletic event that promotes nervousness. It is also the lack of socialization and understanding by our Black athletes and Black culture of what responsibilities coincide with athletic success. Our Black athletes need to understand that they must become bilingual. They can speak the language of our Black culture when it is appropriate, but they must also be capable of speaking the King's English when necessary.

To help with this distinction our athletes must have clinics (similar to a coach or referee clinic) where they are taught social and communication skills. Instead of watching films of jump shots and dunks the athletes should be shown interviews and press conferences of players and coaches. For example, Michael Jordan's first press conference with the Washington DC media when he was introduced as part owner and President of Basketball Operations for the Washington Wizards should be mandatory viewing for Black youth. Not only should it be shown for the articulate, poised, calm, thoughtful and insightful presence and answers Jordan provided, but also for the fact that a Black man was now part owner of a professional basketball team.

Other press conferences with sports figures such as "Magic" Johnson, part owner of the Los Angles Lakers, should be part of the course for learning how to handle situations with the media. Game interviews with basketball superstars such as Vince Carter of the Toronto Raptors, Alonzo Mourning of the Miami Heat, David Robinson of the San Antonio Spurs, Shaquille O'Neal and Kobe Bryant of the Los Angeles Lakers and many more from other sports should be part of the training classes. The course should have the young Black athletes involved with role-playing as the media and the athlete. Video taping and constructive criticism of the dialog should be mandatory.

The Black athlete and the Black community is so entrenched with its relationship to basketball that many other opportunities for scholarships to college are passing by without a notice or a care. The Black athlete and Black community are determined, prideful, and single-minded about the philosophy that basketball, football, and track are our domain and we have exclusivity and an undeniable right to play these sports. Yet with exposure, access, and opportunity the same circumstances that led us to dominate in basketball and football can and should make us successful in other sports as well. However, our narrow thinking and primary obsession with basketball and football have us competing against ourselves for the relatively few scholarships offered each year in those sports. The other result is that we eliminate ourselves from consideration for athletic scholarships and opportunities available in other sports such as soccer and lacrosse.

There is an abundance of opportunities for college tuition assistance and partial and full scholarships to universities in this country to play other sports besides basketball and football. Yet, for plenty of reasons Black athletes, especially in the big city, avoid sports such as volleyball, tennis, lacrosse, golf, soccer, and others that provide scholarship opportunities to college.

The *Washington Post's* selection of the spring 2000 high school All-Metropolitan athletes provides a prime illustration of the lack of participation by Black athletes in sports other than basketball and football. Of nine highlighted sports, including men's and women's lacrosse, swimming, softball, baseball, tennis, gymnastics, track and field, soccer and men's golf, the only sport where Black athletes excelled was track and field, a sport where Black athletes have been channeled for decades. In the remaining eight sports, of the over 125 athletes accorded first team honors in their respective sports, less than 10 were Black athletes.

By contrast, the *Post's* 2001 All-Metropolitan men and womens basketball first-team featured 19 Black athletes out of 20 players. The disparity of numbers is based on several dynamics. First, the Black community is quite content to channel our athletes toward basketball and football. We, as parents see the success and domination of the college and professional athletes on television. We promote that road to our youth, and often wish for them to emulate that athletic path. We relate our own past personal accomplishments with the two sports that we easily share with our sons and daughters. With the proliferation and year-round access to the sports, particularly basketball, it is easy and convenient to have youth participate and subsequently believe that a professional future is possible.

Our youth are captivated by the "living large" status of professional basketball and football stars and are easily sold on the merits of the game without a glance at other sports. Our school systems in Black communities are faced with budget cuts and barely have adequate funding to carry football and basketball teams, much less other sports programs. Then, when they do offer other sports, the students demonstrate only a half-hearted and lukewarm endorsement and commitment to participate. Consequently, if parents want to have their children compete in other sports, they must transfer to distant schools or a private school. They can also enroll the student in outside special programs and instructional classes similar to piano lessons that are expensive and out of the mainstream of high school competition, thus limiting scholarship opportunities.

The bottom line is that our Black culture, with its self-imposed limitations and disdain for other sports, combined with the lack of funding sources and educational advances from our schools, funnels our athletes to compete exclusively in basketball and football. This ensures a Darwinian struggle for scholarships to college. When I am asked why the Black athlete dominates basketball, I just as quickly ask why White athletes dominate golf. The answer is exactly the same, "Exposure, access, culture, opportunity, and money".

One of the easiest yet the most important way to educate and relate to young people is to have a presence. Whether you have a child or not, Black adults, and especially Black men, need to stand as role models, as leaders of the community, and as concerned and caring guiding lights for the interest and welfare of our youth. The connection will be invaluable to both youth and adult.

It can start with as small a gesture as attending an athletic event in the neighborhood. Adults need to incorporate into their busy schedule an attempt to watch a weeknight high school basketball game or Saturday afternoon football game. The sheer presence of adults in attendance will resonate among the students, players, and school administrators as they feel that somebody cares enough to take an interest in them. Attending an athletic event will energize the youth, but it will also prove to be an enlightening and invigorating experience for the adult, especially for those that have read too many negative newspaper headlines and have distanced themselves from community youth involvement.

Adults that attend high school events are watching sports competition at its purest form. Athletes compete for sheer pleasure without the bright lights and big business aura that defines the college and professional game. It is an inexpensive and family oriented evening. It is a short ride to a local school without parking issues. It is a fast-paced, high energy, spirited event usually lasting less than two hours in which adults can see the excellence of our youth on display both in the stands and on the floor or field.

In fact, once seated among the students, adults need to take the opportunity to dialog with them. Solicit conversation and interaction with the youth. Ask them questions. It is a guarantee that adults will find that young people have a lot to say and will appreciate the opportunity to exchange thoughts with an adult. Youth are engaging, insightful, humorous, and bright. The problems that adults hear about youth on the newscasts that force them to lock their doors and abandon community involvement will dissipate and be replaced with bridge-building and understanding. Indeed, distrust and apprehension will be replaced with an accurate acknowledgement that most of our youth are on the right path, albeit against tough and difficult odds.

Balance is the operative word. The Black community and Black athlete must find the proper balance and perspective with sports.

Often, we as Black parents and concerned adults take our community's most precious resource—our young Black males—and confirm them as athletes first. We allow them to establish and elevate their status solely by their skills on the basketball court. As Black parents and concerned adults, we allow this to happen when we swell with pride and celebration at their on-the-court accomplishments and shamefully anticipate future NBA success. Even if we do not encourage the NBA dream in word, we do it in deed. We often feed our athlete an unbalanced diet of year round pursuit of basketball though AAU, the bartering with private schools for his and her athletic talents, by transferring to three or more high schools in pursuit of the "right" hoops home, and eventually, by negotiating with college recruiters for athletic benefits and perks. All the while we are promoting the subtle statement that education is grudgingly necessary but clearly secondary.

Many will point to the Black community's obsession with getting its athletes to the NBA as a prime example of how balance is lost. It is too simplistic a cry. Somewhere along the way the Black community in general and the Black sports culture, in particular, have made the NBA dream an either-or proposition. It need not be that way. Our athletes should be taught the many goals and dreams that can be accomplished through a college education. While they may pale in comparison to the NBA, they must still be stressed to our youth. However, what ultimately turns off our youth to other goals and dreams is that alternative professions are often presented as a replacement for pursing a NBA goal, instead of in conjunction with a professional sports career. The former is born of negativity and low expectation, of believing our youth can't achieve an NBA career and must focus on another unspecific goal. The latter path expresses confidence that our youth can and should have multiple goals and dreams and that it is possible to achieve them all. Our youth can detect the difference in the presentation.

When we, as parents and concerned adults, allow the pendulum of our emotions and high athletic dreams for our youth to swing heavily toward the NBA, we are unconsciously setting a bar of low expectation for our young athletes, for ourselves, and our communities. The NBA dream is fine. But funneling our athlete toward that dream while abdicating the importance of God, family and ethnic pride, and community obligation is wrong. Failing to encourage and inspire multiple dreams of success off the court and stressing the independence derived from education and the college degree does a tremendous disservice to him. Our Black athletes and Black youth are capable of reaching many goals.

Lastly, but most importantly our Black youth must come to know that they are not a mistake. God created the universe and made man in His perfect image and that includes Black people.

SOURCES

By far, most of the material in this book came from my interviews, discussions and meetings with high school, college, and professional players, AAU, youth league, college, current and former coaches, parents, teachers, school and university administrators, alumni, media people, referees, colleagues, and friends, many of whom are named in the Acknowledgment section of the book.

The statistical data used in the book was provided by *1999 NCAA Division I Graduation Rates Report* (The National Collegiate Athletic Association), *2001 NCAA Division I Graduation Rates Report* (www.ncaa.org), *The Insider's Guide to the Colleges 2002, Compiled and edited by the staff of the Yale Daily News* (The Yale Daily News Publishing Company, Inc.), *The Princeton Review Complete Book of Colleges 2002 Edition, Random House, Inc.* 1998 Racial and Gender Report Card, 2001 Racial and Gender Report Card (Northeastern University Sport In Society), The Sporting News College Basketball, Fall 1997, 1998, 1999, 2000, 2001.

Other reference materials included Georgetown Basketball 1999-2000 Official Hoya Game day Program: The John Thompson Story, *How to Play the Sports Recruiting Game and Get an Athletic Scholarship: The Handbook and Guide to Success for the African American High School Student Athlete*, Rodney J. McKissic (Amber Books), *The History of Our United States* 3rd Edition (A Beka Book A Ministry of Pensacola Christian College), *And The Walls Came Tumbling Down* Frank Fitzpatrick (Simon &Schuster), *Darwin's Athletes: How Sport has Damaged Black America and Preserved the Myth of Race* John Hoberman (Houghton Mifflin Company), *College Sports Inc.: The Athletic Department vs. The University* Murray Sperber (Henry Holt and Company) *Sole Influence: Basketball, Corporate Greed, and the Corruption of America's Youth* Dan Wetzel and Don Yaeger (Warner Books Inc.).